Debra

High-Impact Management

Solutions for Today's Busy Public-Sector Managers

Lisa Haneberg

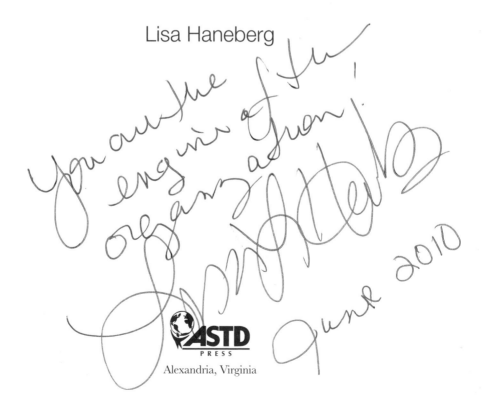

You are the engine of the organization!

[signature] June 2010

ASTD PRESS

Alexandria, Virginia

ASTD Press is an internationally renowned source of insightful and practical information on workplace learning and performance topics, including training basics, evaluation and return-on-investment, instructional systems development, e-learning, leadership, and career development. Visit our website at www.astd.org.

Ordering information: Books published by ASTD Press can be purchased by visiting ASTD's website at store.astd.org or by calling 800.628.2783 or 703.683.8100.

Library of Congress Control Number: 2009940086

ISBN-10: 1-56286-699-0
ISBN-13: 978-1-56286-699-0

ASTD Press Editorial Staff:
Director of Content: Dean Smith
Manager, ASTD Press: Jacqueline Edlund-Braun
Senior Associate Editor: Tora Estep
Senior Associate Editor: Justin Brusino
Editorial Assistant: Victoria DeVaux

Copyeditor: Alfred Imhoff
Indexer: April Michelle Davis
Proofreader: Kris Patenaude
Interior Design and Production: Kathleen Schaner
Cover Design: Steve Fife
Cover Art: Digital Vision

Printed by Versa Press, Inc., East Peoria, Illinois, www.versapress.com

To all the government superheroes out there, leading from the middle, and making an impact while swallowing a fire hose dose of to-do list items.

Contents

Introduction: Middle Management—Magic or Mayhem?.................... 1

1   The High-Impact Middle Management System............................ 5
2   How to Think Like a High-Impact Manager............................... 17
3   Power Partnerships 31
4   The Reality Check: Measuring Current Performance 43
5   Using the High-Impact Management Playbook
    to Facilitate Peak Performance 63
6   Mucky-Muck Obstructions: Navigating the Obstacle Course 75
7   Organizational Alignment: Ensuring That the Department
    Delivers Results... 93
8   High-Impact Leaders Are Unstoppable! Wiping Out Limitations
    to Results 105
9   Using High-Impact Management to Make the Most of
    Your Busy Day.. 129
10 Coaching: Helping Others Achieve Breakthroughs 147
11 Coachability: How to Reach Goals Faster and Better................. 159
12 The High-Impact Management System: Putting It
    Together for Maximum Managerial Flow.................................. 167

Appendix: Additional Resources and Recommended Reading.......... 173

Tell Me What You Think.. 178

About the Author 179

Index 181

Middle Management— Magic or Mayhem?

In any organization, there are two kinds of managers. There are those who get the work done but never think beyond what needs to be completed in the short term. They rush from one task to another, never quite recognizing which is most important to their agency's larger objectives. Though they may work hard and have good intentions, they fail to see the big picture and, thus, add little value to their organization or the functions they manage. Then there are high-impact managers. These managers see the big picture. They know how to manage operational practices and execute tactical goals to support strategic initiatives. They add value to their organization and thus elevate their position from that of an intermediary to key player.

There is an almost magical synergy in a work environment when high-impact managers operate at peak efficiency. Their questions are timely and on target; their ideas are provocative in ways that help move the work forward. They know how to think and act strategically. Transitions from one task to the next seem choreographed. As they walk through the office, their demeanor is calm but they have a sense of urgency. Busy, focused, and driven, these managers produce results and imbue the workplace with energy. Those who watch these managers may feel motivated or intimidated—but they are not unaffected.

Although their days are full, they have more time at their disposal than other managers who produce less. That's because these effective middle managers use tiny pockets of time to accomplish big things. They plan well and anticipate challenges coming their way. When they do make a mistake, they quickly solve the problem and learn from the experience. These managers are effective because they understand what they need to do, methodically do those things, and adjust quickly and proactively when barriers pop up or conditions change.

Unfortunately, many managers have never experienced this kind of productivity. They spend their days trying to catch up, never mind moving ahead. Barriers and challenges bring their productivity to a grinding halt. They focus on the urgent rather than the important. Disconnected by a lack of communication with their peers and managers, their work is no longer aligned to achieve results, and team members lose sight of how their work influences the organization or why it even matters. Results suffer because the manager and his or her team are not set up to deliver them.

Nothing is more heartbreaking than seeing smart, hardworking, and well-meaning managers fail. But in today's ever-changing and competitive work environment, it happens all too often. Success is most difficult for middle managers because their role is more complicated and challenging than the roles of either frontline supervisors or senior leaders. Even so, middle managers can experience peak performance with the right guidance, development, and support. To do so, they need to learn the craft of middle management and overcome several challenges that can wreck their capacity to perform.

A great middle manager—referred to in this book as a *high-impact manager*—is an individual who makes substantial qualitative and quantitative contributions to his or her organization and moves work forward with velocity—speed and direction. The high-impact manager can straddle several planning periods to address the needs of today, this week, this month, this year, and the next few years. He or she understands the difficult and complex nature of his or her role and feels energized by being the conduit between agency thought, action, and results. High-impact managers "get it." They know that their job is the most exciting one for those who relish being in the thick of it.

This book offers a vision of high-impact management for public employees and a system for achieving this superior level of performance. This High-Impact Management System has been created to provide busy middle managers with an integrated set of practices and techniques that will enable them to maximize their results and success. It is a distinct system because it addresses systemwide execution and success from the perspective of middle management, recognizes that middle management is the engine for results, and offers regimens and practices to ensure performance.

Who Is a Middle Manager?

Depending on the size of the organization, middle managers may hold the title of director, department head, administrator, or manager. Middle management positions are responsible leadership posts typically two to seven layers below the top level of senior leadership. In city or county governments, for example, middle management typically starts with department heads and includes several layers of the organization chart to senior supervisors. They may have other supervisors or managers reporting to them and are responsible for managing at least one function or program. Middle managers are high enough on the organization chart that they are expected to understand and take part in creating project and program plans, budgets, and other planning documents.

The Motivation for This Book

Middle managers have a more direct impact on results than any other layer of an organization; it is vital, therefore, that they receive the resources and development they need. Sadly, there are few books or training programs targeted to meet the unique needs of middle managers. This is unacceptable and a serious concern, because organizations suffer when middle managers do not know what to do. As the glue that connects strategies and goals to work productivity, middle managers can either enable or impede accomplishments.

This book is one of the few that explains and illustrates successful high-impact management practices and tools. Its goal is to share this system of management in a way that is clear and easy to implement. Middle managers who incorporate this system into their daily practices will receive a payoff of improved management skills, better results, and increased promotability. Implementing high-impact management will enable you to enjoy your job more fully, see better results, and experience peak performance from yourself and your team.

The Special Challenges for Public-Sector Managers

Being a middle manager for a government organization is a tough job! In addition to the challenges faced by all middle managers, public-sector managers need to lead and manage in a work environment that is more complex and thick with regulations and constraints. You might have little authority to make changes, and it is often harder to change processes and make decisions in lumbering government organizations. The suggestions included in this book have been selected because of their potential to help public-sector managers, and I have included many stories and examples from government managers. I have also shared several examples from the for-profit world that are applicable or transferrable to the public sector. I love working with government managers because the work you do is in some ways arguably even more important than the work done by your private-sector counterparts—when governments work well, everyone wins.

How the Book Is Organized

This book offers a comprehensive look at the challenges and opportunities that middle managers face today. Each chapter addresses a dimension, or layer, of the middle manager's job. Although the information in each chapter can be read and applied separately, you will find the techniques to be complementary and additive. The more you try and use them, the greater your results will be. Please enjoy the book's chapters in the order that best addresses your needs; however, I do recommend reading chapters 1 and 2 before the other chapters, because it explains the foundations and assumptions of the High-Impact Management System.

The High-Impact Management System

The numbers were in. Black & Decker had regained the market share it had lost over the past several years—and then some. The company's new DeWalt line of power tools had made it to the marketplace in record time and had received rave reviews. It was a great lineup. The tools represented cutting-edge technology, and they were beautifully designed and expertly packaged. Cross-functional international product development teams had worked tirelessly on the DeWalt line design, development, and launch for more than two years. And now their hard work had really paid off for Black & Decker, giving it the boost in the marketplace that they sorely needed. Everyone involved in the DeWalt launch knew they had been part of something special.

It would be hard to argue that the DeWalt vision and strategy for producing a superior line of tools for the serious do-it-yourselfer and the professional were not brilliant; they set the stage for the right work to happen. The inspiring strategy got the team started, but what made the DeWalt plan's execution so successful was the quality of Black & Decker's middle managers. In the end, it was high-impact managers who produced breakthrough results and put Black & Decker back on the map as a major player in the competitive do-it-yourself power tool market. How did they do it?

- They were extraordinarily good project managers.
- They had an uncompromising attitude about hiring only the best for the DeWalt team.
- They practiced effective cross-functional and international communication. They built relationships before they needed them.
- They established an environment that encouraged creativity and innovation.
- They planned well and made sure that priorities were crystal clear.
- They communicated the vision of the senior executives with passion and clarity.

Black & Decker's team of high-impact managers did outstanding work and made a significant contribution to a companywide achievement. That is high-impact management in action.

What Middle Managers Do

Middle managers are the fundamental link joining an organization's strategies to the people and projects needed to produce results. They are the folks in the middle who see and manage how various parts of the organization work. It's a big and often underestimated responsibility. Figure 1-1 shows what the typical middle manager's role might look like. In the top portion of the figure, various concerns converge and compete for a middle manager's time and attention. These concerns include a broad range of tasks such as planning, goal setting, performance management, problem solving, process improvement, relationship building, analysis, communication updates, budgeting, and decision making. Barriers and mucky-muck (see chapter 6) can block these items from getting the time and consideration they deserve.

The funnel represents the distillation process that middle managers must use to decide how they will spend time and complete their work. Middle managers are like a department funnel, interpreting and translating strategies, needs, and choices so their teams can perform. They

Figure 1-1. The Typical Middle Manager's Role

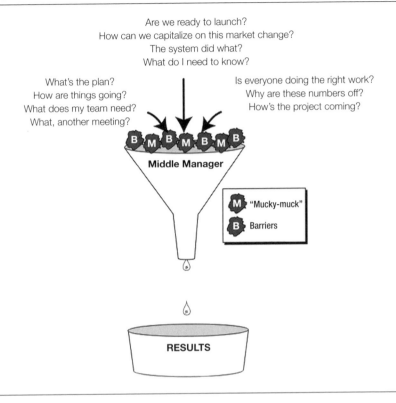

practice techniques and make decisions that influence results. Ineffective work practices and a preponderance of barriers can combine to slow output to a trickle.

Figure 1-2 shows what results can look like when managers use the High-Impact Management System. The results are much better! High-impact management helps middle managers deal with daily tasks and strategic demands while providing tools to reduce barriers to productivity. Middle management areas of concern that high-impact management addresses include

- paradigms that best serve execution and results
- fostering collaboration to improve results and efficiency
- determining team performance
- goal setting for peak performance

Figure 1-2. A Middle Manager Using High-Impact Management Techniques

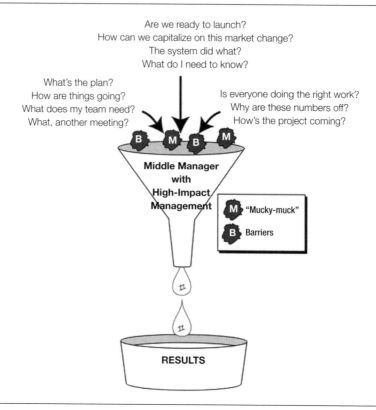

- dealing with daily obstacles to results
- removing factors that limit throughput
- time management
- process alignment techniques
- performance management techniques
- skills for coaching others
- using the High-Impact Management System to improve results
- honing middle management skills to build your career.

By using high-impact management, you will save time and resources by focusing your efforts in areas where they will have the greatest impact. In addition, this book presents a number of techniques that can facilitate breakthroughs—those quantum leap improvements that can happen quickly and reignite results.

The Guiding Principles of the High-Impact Management System

Every management system is built on a set of assumptions and principles. These values form the foundation for each philosophy, technique, and tool included in the system. The High-Impact Management System was designed with eight basic principles in mind. These principles speak to what is unique about middle management and how public-sector middle managers produce great results. These guiding principles apply to organizations of any size or in any industry. In addition to providing a theoretical backdrop for the system, the guiding principles of high-impact management are powerful catalytic tools when used as part of a middle manager's definition of success (see chapter 2). Let's look at each principle.

Principle 1: Being a Middle Manager Is Exciting

In almost any organization, the most challenging and rewarding jobs will be in middle management. Why? Because middle managers are close to the action, but they also take part in shaping the future strategy and direction of the agency. Top executives rarely get to see the action in which middle managers take part, and they also must deal with more bureaucracy and politics. Frontline managers get to see the action but rarely help determine the agency's future. As a middle manager you have your finger on the pulse of the workplace and can make things happen. Senior executives trust talented middle managers to implement the organization's vision and mission. And because there are generally several layers of middle management, you can enjoy the benefits of this fascinating work while progressing in your career.

Principle 2: Middle Management Is a Craft

The middle manager's job is complex and dynamic, and thus requires focus to deliver results. Weighing competing demands and making choices about how to manage time takes practice and development. Navigating and managing emotionally charged work relationships is a learned skill that requires diplomacy and finesse. As managers grow and mature, they hone their craft and create a style that is effective and unique to them. Along the way, they also learn techniques and practices via mentoring, training, and coaching. The purpose of this book is to help you hone your management skills.

Principle 3: Great Managers Do What Others Don't or Won't

A middle manager's job is littered with tasks that are undesirable, tiring, mundane, or even frightening. Great managers do things that others put off, procrastinate, or ignore. Mediocre managers don't. Not everyone likes to counsel employees or create work plans, but these tasks are necessary and time sensitive.

Principle 4: Beliefs Determine Behavior

Managers act on what they think about most and believe to be true. Their actions come from a set of beliefs formed about job responsibilities, expectations, and reinforcement. To create a different result, you need to adopt a different mindset. Breakthroughs can occur when beliefs line up with efforts to achieve the desired outcome.

Principle 5: Relationships Influence Results

Relationships developed with team members, peers, managers, and customers are important. If you discount relationships, you won't garner the cooperation and support you need from others to produce ideal results—and you are more likely to see your career derail. Great managers develop and maintain positive relationships. Managers who are poor team players or unpleasant to work with are less successful. Many eventually lose their jobs, and most will not progress far. The old admonition rings true here: Never burn your bridges.

Principle 6: Managerial Strengths and Weaknesses Are Known

People notice who is charismatic, who gets defensive, and whether someone is likely to pass the buck. Management is public work, and it is noticed by employees and coworkers. Everyone knows who is the best negotiator and who is the underperformer. Because strengths and weaknesses are known, there is no disadvantage to openly discussing them. As a manager you have a choice to make. You can take an interest in and deal with your development needs, or you can ignore them and hope no one notices. But the latter strategy is flawed because people *do* notice. The only practical and helpful approach is to see faults and failings for what they are and openly discuss them so improvement can occur. You don't want to be the last to know if you have a habit that is driving people nuts or derailing the work. Those managers who acknowledge improvement areas will enjoy more support and respect from others than will those who do not.

Principle 7: Great Middle Management Can Be Learned, but One Must "Get It"

Middle management is a craft, a set of practices, and a job that managers can learn with the right training and guidance. Good middle managers are cultivated, not born. Great managers come in wildly different styles and personalities. However, it is essential that all middle managers fully understand their jobs and responsibilities. Managers who don't take on their role are not likely to succeed and will often see their careers stall or dwindle.

Principle 8: Middle Managers Exist to Make Things Happen

High-impact middle managers are not there to oversee what is going to occur on its own. They make a huge difference and play a vital role in improving the organization. It is in the face of defeat, during an impending failure, or on the verge of an exciting opportunity that a middle manager's role kicks into high gear. Great middle managers know they exist to make a positive difference and seek out opportunities to make an impact.

Summing Up

These eight guiding principles are reinforced throughout the High-Impact Management System and this book. High-impact management is for professional managers who are interested in new or different techniques that will make their work more fruitful and who want to make a difference.

High-Impact Management Generates Results

High-impact management builds middle management capacity by developing results-oriented responses (RORs), which are enablers that can have an immediate effect on work. Each high-impact management component reinforces and supports the others so that as you integrate them into your management regimen, the results will improve at a more significant rate than if you had implemented them separately. As you develop your ability to apply RORs in one area, you will also learn skills that will enable you to handle other tasks more effectively. For example, developing dialogue skills for goal setting will also aid you in your ability to use dialogue to improve processes. An ROR is not a technique in itself, but it influences how a technique is used.

Table 1-1 lists several of the RORs used by high-impact managers. The results will vary, depending on the choices made about what to do and how to spend time. The RORs are listed on the left side of the table, and low-results responses are listed on the right side. The RORs produce better results. Managers who are dissatisfied with their results can look through this table to discover how to improve their responses.

These RORs can help you focus your time and energy where it will yield the highest benefits (see the 80/20 rule later in this chapter). A quick review of the list of RORs can help get a stalled project or goal moving again. RORs, guiding principles, and a respect for the important and complex nature of the middle manager's job are central to the High-Impact Management System. They come together to help middle managers improve their performance, results, and career success.

How to Apply RORs to Everyday Middle Management Challenges

Steve struggled to understand why the marketing materials produced by his department did not capture the essence of his agency's products. He

Table 1-1. Results-Oriented Responses Cheat Sheet

Results-oriented responses are listed on the left side of the model and low-results responses on the right side. Responses on the left side produce better results. Managers dissatisfied with their results can look through the model to discover how to improve their responses.

Results-Oriented Responses	Low-Results Responses
Being an owner: Assumes responsibility for the outcome. Takes initiative to make things better. Does whatever it takes to get ideal results. Heart is committed and mind is engaged.	**Being a custodian:** Does only what is required. Waits for others to act. Hopes someone else will take ownership. Avoids that which is unpleasant. Behavior is compliant. Heart and mind not fully engaged.
Being active: Takes the initiative to get things done. Is not easily deterred by setbacks. Proactive. When barriers are present, immediately identifies them and implements an alternative action plan.	**Being passive:** Won't take action unless told to do so. Acts only when necessary. Reactive in stance and style. Barriers and setbacks result in inaction.
Generating: Able to generate new and better alternative approaches and carry them out. Creates from unlimited possibilities. Does not get stuck on how things are already being done.	**Being automatic:** Sticks with the way things have always been done, preserves the status quo. Prefers to act by habit and won't move out of his/her comfort zone. Does not create new approaches or solutions.
Keeping promises: Does what is promised. Fulfills commitments. Keeps his or her word.	**Broken promises or commitments:** Does not follow through with what he or she has promised or committed to. Lets to-do items build up beyond the date expected. Does not follow through on real or implied agreements.
Influencing through enrollment: Influences others by having them see, understand, and take ownership of the goal for themselves. Demonstrates the strategy and plan in such a way that others see and take on the vision for themselves. Others are committed and passionate about the vision and plan.	**Influencing through subtle coercion:** Communicates the vision and plan in a way that resembles a direction or a suggestion. Influences others by making them feel they need to accept and conform. This type of influencing others rarely results in committed and passionate performance.
Being service oriented: Sees his or her role as one that provides service to others. Facilitates cooperation, commitment, and learning. Manages from the mindset, "What can I do to help others excel today?"	**Expecting to be served:** Sees his or her role as one in which people should serve him or her. This stance limits the capacity to have impact on others. Manages from the mindset, "What have you done for me today?"

(continued on next page)

Table 1-1. Results-Oriented Responses Cheat Sheet (continued)

Results-Oriented Responses	Low-Results Responses
Being coachable: Accepts and uses feedback, input, criticism, and ideas from others and is curiously observant. Is not defensive when given feedback. Recognizes that others have something to offer.	**Being uncoachable:** Blocks the environment from being influential, puts up barriers. Focuses more on being right, looking good, and appearing in charge.
Practicing quality dialogue: Communicates with the intent of making a difference or moving a topic forward. Engages in active conversation focused on the topic at hand.	**Using dialogue without purpose:** Communicates in a way that does not move the topic forward. Spends time discussing rumors, gossip, complaints, diversions, whining, and opinions not helpful toward enabling the desired result.

Source: Adapted from *H.I.M.M. (High Impact Middle Management): Solutions for Today's Busy Managers,* by Lisa Haneberg. More information is available in chapter 1, or visit www.lisahaneberg.com.

was also frustrated by the fact that while his team members always seemed busy, they were not completing the most important work—ensuring the quality of the materials. Was the writing compelling enough? Were the pictures good enough? Did the layout convey the right message? All of these areas were part of the problem, but the underlying cause of the quality problem was less specific. How was Steve approaching the problem? Were his responses likely to lead to success or failure? Reviewing just a few items on the list of RORs sheds some light on his situation:

- Being an owner: Steve owned his role as functional leader, but he also let the fact that he had inherited the process slow down his efforts to improve it. There was an opportunity for him to improve results by taking more ownership of how he wanted the department to run currently, rather than going with the status quo.
- Being active: Steve had implemented a few small ideas and new actions. However, he would be able to realize more significant improvements if he would take action in a more meaningful way.
- Generating: Steve was a very creative manager, so generating new ideas would not have been a problem—if it hadn't been for

the issue of people. He was allowing his preconceptions of what the current team players would accept or reject to curtail his natural tendency to be a creative problem solver.

By looking at just three RORs, Steve could create several potential approaches for how to improve the production process. High-impact management uses the elegant simplicity of the RORs as a basis for each specific technique. As you review each suggestion, you can return to the list of RORs in table 1-1 and see how it ties into at least one preferred response.

The 80/20 Rule

In the early 1900s, the economist Vilfredo Pareto established the Pareto Principle, otherwise known as the 80/20 rule. He found that 20 percent of the population owned 80 percent of the land in Italy. He then noticed that this ratio applied to other things in science, business, and life. The 80/20 rule asserts that in any given situation, 20 percent of the work performed will account for 80 percent of the results. Conversely, the other 80 percent of the work will yield only 20 percent of the results. Thus, a few actions will make a greater proportional impact. The 80/20 rule is also used to evaluate errors and problems; therefore, the top 20 percent of systemic problems causes 80 percent of the inefficiencies.

The High-Impact Management System applies the 80/20 rule to many aspects of middle management. Thus, just a few methods practiced together will have a significant impact on results and execution. High-impact management focuses on the 20 percent of the effort that will yield 80 percent of the impact for busy middle managers, and highlights the 20 percent of actions that matter most.

The High-Impact Management System was built on the premise that a middle manager's job is challenging, complex, and very important to an organization's success. As a middle manager, you have the opportunity to do work that is meaningful and exciting. The right training and development can help frustrated or unsuccessful middle managers become high-impact managers. Unfortunately, most middle managers are so busy and overwhelmed that they are not likely to take the time to attend training classes. That is a shame, because mastering middle management is much easier with good coaching and guidance. The High-Impact Management System presented in this book will teach time-pressed middle managers what they can do differently that will offer the greatest benefit to their team and their organization.

....

How to Think Like a High-Impact Manager

How a middle manager approaches a situation can either help or hinder the results he or she is seeking. Thoughts and beliefs can limit opportunities or, conversely, enable options to be discovered and considered. High-impact managers select beliefs that support their goals. When your thinking is aligned with the larger objective, productive actions naturally happen and lead to positive results.

Success Stories

Many well-known success stories illustrate the power of aligning beliefs with goals. A belief may seem like a tiny inconsequential thing, but it can get an organization rolling in the right direction. The reverse is also true. Stagnant thinking that is not aligned with goals can contribute to the downfall of an organization or department. Let's look at a few examples of successful leaders who recognized the importance of beliefs and how those beliefs make an impact on results.

More Than Sausage

"If it is to be, it is up to me. If it is up to me, it shall be." Thousands of managers have heard Ralph Stayer, the CEO of Johnsonville Foods, say these words during talks at organizations around the world. Johnsonville Foods has enjoyed significant and lasting success with Stayer at the helm. The company is famous for its bottom-up, top-down integration of ownership and innovation that creates the best and most popular sausage products on the market today.

In his best-selling business book *Flight of the Buffalo: Soaring to Excellence, Learning to Let Employees Lead*, Stayer describes the importance of productive thoughts and the breakthroughs he experienced by aligning his beliefs for success: "I learned to change from being a victim to being responsible by asking myself, 'What am I doing or not doing that causes the situation I don't like?' Restating the problem into factors that I control helps me feel, and be, powerful." Part of Stayer's leadership mantra is to first assume that "I am the problem" and then approach each improvement opportunity from there.

Direct to You

In his book *Direct from Dell*, Michael Dell wrote:

> Our success is due, in part, to not just an ability, but a willingness, to look at things differently. I believe opportunity is part instinct and part immersion—in an industry, a subject, or an area of expertise. Dell is proof that people can learn to recognize and take advantage of opportunities that others are convinced don't exist. You don't have to be a genius, or a visionary, or even a college graduate to think unconventionally. You just need a framework and a dream.

Michael Dell started his computer company in 1984 with $1,000 and a dream to one day be as big as IBM. By 1998, the Dell Computer Corporation was taking in $12 million in sales over the Internet each day; and by 2003, it was number 36 on the *Fortune* 500 list. The Dell business model changed the way all computer manufacturers do business, including how they go to market, manage inventory, and produce products.

Delivery You Can Count On

"Back in 1971 my belief was that you could run these small, high-value-added computer parts through this hub-and-spoke system. Also, I did something else a little bit unusual, which was to combine the airplanes and trucks into one delivery system. This didn't seem to me to be so controversial, but all the traditional people felt that it was highly iconoclastic. So that's the genesis of Federal Express." This is how Fred Smith, CEO of FedEx, described the thinking behind this successful business launch in 1971 in a recent *Fortune* magazine article.

Over the last three decades, FedEx has revolutionized the shipping business. Smith believed the shipping business could work in the same way banks clear checks: through a hub-and-spoke system. By applying this model to shipping, FedEx delivered on a promise of service consistency, speed, and accuracy. Since the launch of FedEx, UPS and the U.S. Postal Service have come out with similar services to match the breadth of shipping choices, reliability, and efficiency that FedEx has achieved.

Turning Beliefs into Results

Each of these stories illustrates how powerful, positive, and focused beliefs lead to favorable results and how thoughts affect actions. By adopting beliefs that served their goals, Stayer, Dell, and Smith produced outstanding results. Successes, a few setbacks, and a drive to continue the move forward characterized their journeys. Some of their beliefs have remained the same, while others have changed as needed to serve their goals. These CEOs know that how they approach running their businesses has contributed to their successes.

When results are lacking, the first thing to look at is the underlying beliefs that are driving actions. The relationship between beliefs and actions is important. Actions come from beliefs, and actions and results reinforce beliefs. This cycle can help or hinder success. Figure 2-1 shows how beliefs get in the way of results. Notice how the cycle reinforces the status quo and increases the manager's levels of stress and frustration.

Figure 2-2 depicts a more productive belief-action cycle. This model shows how helpful beliefs lead to productive actions and improved results. These results reinforce proactive and positive beliefs. The difference between those beliefs that serve a manager's goals and those that do not is easy to distinguish when both are examined closely.

Figure 2-1. A Typical Belief-Action Cycle

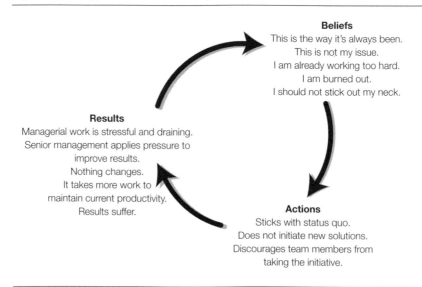

Beliefs
This is the way it's always been.
This is not my issue.
I am already working too hard.
I am burned out.
I should not stick out my neck.

Results
Managerial work is stressful and draining.
Senior management applies pressure to
improve results.
Nothing changes.
It takes more work to
maintain current productivity.
Results suffer.

Actions
Sticks with status quo.
Does not initiate new solutions.
Discourages team members from
taking the initiative.

Figure 2-2. The High-Impact Management Belief-Action Cycle

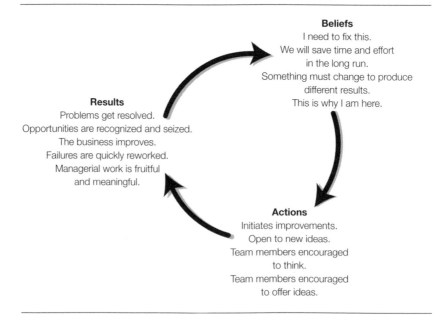

Beliefs
I need to fix this.
We will save time and effort
in the long run.
Something must change to produce
different results.
This is why I am here.

Results
Problems get resolved.
Opportunities are recognized and seized.
The business improves.
Failures are quickly reworked.
Managerial work is fruitful
and meaningful.

Actions
Initiates improvements.
Open to new ideas.
Team members encouraged
to think.
Team members encouraged
to offer ideas.

High-impact managers get better results by taking on a set of beliefs—called a *definition of success*—that will be most useful and by abandoning those beliefs or mindsets that will not serve them well. All managers have a definition of success and it is important to know whether your definition of success is helping you and your team get where you want to go or getting in the way. High-impact managers have a definition of success that leads to ideal results and personal satisfaction.

Examining Your Inner Beliefs

People spend most of their waking hours in conversation—not with others—but with themselves. The mind, on both the conscious and unconscious levels, is constantly processing internal chatter, or "self-talk." The internal dialogue that is most critical for a manager is that regarding the beliefs they hold about accomplishment and failure.

These messages are particularly powerful because they shape the choices you make and how you look at your job. Imagine what would happen if you believed that being strong meant winning arguments at any cost. You would probably act like an obnoxious control freak and alienate others. This would not yield good results. If another middle manager adopted the belief that disagreements should be handled in a manner that preserves and strengthens relationships, he or she would approach things differently, and the results would be more productive. When managers examine and realign their definition of success, they can experience improved results and perhaps an immediate breakthrough.

What Is Your Definition of Success?

Your definition of success is the collection of beliefs you hold that affects how you choose to manage. These beliefs determine how you will approach making decisions, including which activities you will tend to favor and which you might avoid. They also influence how you react during times of stress, failure, success, and creativity. They include

- beliefs about how success is achieved
- beliefs about what success looks like
- beliefs about what is expected
- beliefs reinforced by past successes and failures

- comparisons about what has made others successful
- beliefs, whether positive or negative, passed on by your role models
- beliefs not admitted or recognized until examined in detail
- beliefs that can be changed instantaneously.

As a middle manager, you should regularly evaluate and realign your definition of success. While this may seem straightforward, the process can be tricky because some beliefs are unknown or not recognized. It is common, for example, to verbally define success as one thing and then behave in a contrary way. Verbally, a manager might say that success means achieving results for the benefit of the department and its employees, while behaviorally he or she indicates that success means being right and in control.

To develop the capacity to recognize the beliefs that make up your definition of success, write down five recent actions and ask, "What beliefs led to these actions?" Be wary of your natural inclination to define logical reasoning as the belief that led to your actions. There are many potential beliefs behind an action, so it is best to identify the possibilities and then select the correct motive—for examples, see exercise 2-1.

People who are always late to meetings may not consciously think, "My time is more important," but there is a belief that is making being late an acceptable action. To change the behavior, a new belief needs to take its place such as, "I am expected to be on time," or "being on time shows respect for my peers."

High-Impact Management Thinking about Success

How do high-impact managers define success? Each middle manager is going to hold beliefs specific to his or her function and current goals, as those elements are unique. Many aspects of middle management, however, are similar across industries and agencies. When observing and talking with high-impact managers, it becomes apparent that they share similar beliefs about what success means and how it can best be achieved. What's more, these same beliefs are often held by successful senior executives. This is important to note because a senior manager's expectations of his

Exercise 2-1. Behaviors and Potential Beliefs

Behavior	Potential Beliefs
Always comes to meetings on time	• Professionals show up to meetings on time. • It is important to respect the time of others. • I am expected to be on time. • If I am late, I will miss something.
Always late to meetings	• Everyone is always late. • It is not important to be on time. • My timetable is more important. • I will not miss anything; this is not worthwhile. • Nobody cares if I am late. • I am too busy to be on time.
Defensive when being given feedback	• I need to prove that I am right. • People who are weak need input and help. • I look bad when others challenge my ideas. • I need to win to feel good. • I do not value the other person's input. • I am embarrassed when challenged in public.
Micromanages	• I am expected to stay on top of the details. • If I do not check up on them, they will not complete the work to my satisfaction. • My employees cannot be trusted. • My employees constantly need my help. • This is what good management looks like. • I would rather work with my employees doing these tasks than spend time doing other tasks.

(continued on next page)

Exercise 2-1. Behaviors and Potential Beliefs (continued)

Behavior	Potential Beliefs
Does not share input in meetings when the agenda is known ahead of time	• I prefer to think things through before commenting. • If he wants my opinion, he will ask me. • I do not want to stick my neck out by sharing my ideas. • This is not my meeting; I am not the leader. • I am not expected to contribute in this meeting.
Regularly discusses ideas and issues with manager	• I am expected to form and share ideas and issues. • My manager wants to hear from me. • I need to make sure my manager knows about the key issues within my area. • Managers should toot their own horn to get noticed.
Communicates with manager only when asked and only on topics asked about	• When it comes to my manager, no news is good news. • Managing on my own is a sign of strength; if I ask my manager to review what's going on, this shows that I am weak and need his help. • My manager is too busy to talk to me; I am not a priority.
Avoids coaching others	• If I talk to her, it will make things worse between us. • The discomfort of the conversation will outweigh any benefits. • She will come around on her own. • I have too many tasks to do that are more important. • I don't want to do this.
Does not hesitate to tackle tough personnel issues or to deal with poor performers	• It is my responsibility to handle this issue—it cannot wait. • Performance can only improve if it is dealt with. • If I say nothing, she will more likely fail in the end. • I am accountable for ensuring that everyone performs; there can be no "deadweight" on the team.

or her middle managers will tend to reflect his or her own beliefs about how success is achieved. An additional benefit of high-impact management thinking is that it will serve middle managers well throughout their career progression. High-impact managers subscribe to these beliefs:

- Middle managers are expected to be accountable and take ownership; high-impact management is built on the philosophy that to achieve results, middle managers need to take ownership of whatever needs to be done. This belief drives proactivity and helps to stave off procrastination.

- Middle managers are expected to make a positive contribution to goals; a middle manager's job is to think creatively and proactively, and take initiative to improve his or her performance and his or her team's performance. This belief reinforces the concept that it is not a middle manager's job to maintain or oversee what would otherwise happen on its own.

- Middle managers should be outstanding role models because they influence the culture and tone of the organization; it is not OK for middle managers to be unprofessional or model undesirable behaviors. You will enjoy more success as a manager if you take your role as a professional seriously and recognize that your team members and peers are watching and emulating you when they decide how they should respond to situations.

- Middle managers need to get results; middle managers who believe that it is their job to execute work and deliver results are more likely to choose results-oriented responses and actions. They are also more apt to value productivity measurements and process improvements as tools to monitor, manage, and enhance results.

- Management is a social as well as an agency function; with every meeting you attend and every conversation in which you participate, there is an opportunity to either add to or detract from the quality of the relationship(s). Middle managers need the support and cooperation of those with whom they work. Operating in isolation will not yield success. Recognizing this fact will help you choose responses that preserve and build relationships rather than those that destroy communication.

- Flexible and nimble teams are more successful; middle managers must have their finger on the pulse of the department and know when changes in approach make sense and would be of benefit. A manager who holds this belief is more open to exploring options and creative solutions and is less likely to become comfortable with the status quo.

- Being a middle manager is to play a key role; middle managers should want to spend most of their time managing and facilitating the work of others. Middle managers who do not believe their job is interesting and desirable will not likely serve themselves, or their organization, well.

- Success means delivering results and managing people to achieve optimal productivity and satisfaction; to be truly effective as a high-impact manager, you must reframe your definition of success. Success should be defined more by accomplishments and less by promotions, status, or other extrinsically motivating factors such as executive perks.

- Good managers are responsive to the ideas and concerns of others; being defensive or combative does not reflect favorably on any manager. Being open and flexible makes one seem more intelligent and talented. If you have the constant need to prove that you are right, you will undermine relationships with your superiors and your subordinates.

This list of beliefs forms a powerful definition of success! However, you will naturally adopt beliefs specific to challenges you are facing. For example, if over the next year the focus needs to be on community development, you will adopt beliefs and create a vision about how to best engage stakeholders and what outstanding community partnership looks like.

Imagine what a workplace would look and feel like if all middle managers took on this definition of success. The atmosphere would be electric, exciting, and highly productive. What a great place to work! Here's the amazing part: You can adopt these beliefs right now and they will begin to work immediately. To make the high-impact management definition of success a part of your daily management regimen, you should review the beliefs listed on the previous pages and create a list of supporting actions you can take today. Do this daily until the practice has become second nature. The High-Impact Management Definition of Success Cheat Sheet and Scorecard described in the appendix to this book will also help you make this definition of success part of your daily regimen. Incorporating these beliefs into your daily and weekly planning will help foster responses that will improve results. For some middle managers, the changes may be so striking that they experience a breakthrough.

Discard Definitions of Success That Produce Failure

In addition to adopting new beliefs that support goals, you may need to discard old beliefs that are not useful or are not serving you well. How do you know if your definition of success is constructive? These questions can help you diagnose whether your current beliefs are helpful or harmful:

1. Are results coming in as expected? If not, why not? What beliefs might be responsible for this shortfall?
2. On average, how much time do you spend being reactive versus being proactive? If you spend more time being reactive, why? What beliefs support a focus on reactivity?
3. Have tasks been pushed aside, delayed, or ignored? If yes, why? What's driving this procrastination?
4. Does feedback or criticism result in a defensive comeback, shutdown of communication, or combative posture? Why is it important to you to be right or to win?
5. Who in the organization is your most positive and powerful role model? What does he or she do that is so effective? Which beliefs would support these behaviors?
6. Are team members satisfied with their jobs? Are they frustrated or burned out? If so, why is this the case, and what is the manager's role in fixing this?
7. How enjoyable is middle management? If it is not satisfying work, why not? Are there new beliefs that you could adopt to improve your job satisfaction and your impact on the organization?

On the basis of your answers to these questions, you can begin to recognize unhelpful beliefs and redesign your definition of success. Your nonproductive beliefs also become apparent when you examine disappointments as they occur. For example, if a project did not go well, do a postmortem to discover why this was the case and to understand the thinking that allowed the failure to occur. Was it a lack of follow-up? Too little research before implementation? Whatever the reasons, the actions that were taken came from supporting beliefs. Did you assume that everyone would do his or her work on time and that follow-up should not be required? Did you believe that the key vendor had done the research and that nothing would likely go wrong? What if you had taken on the belief that frequent follow-up meetings would be helpful in keeping everyone on track and uncovering areas where the project could get derailed? Would the results have been any different? Yes, they certainly would have.

Besides the definition of success presented above, you, as a middle manager, can define the beliefs that will best serve your goals by completing this exercise:

1. Create a list of management goals for the coming year. These goals should spell out important accomplishments, key initiatives, and areas that will need special managerial attention.

2. For each goal, identify beliefs that would support success. In other words, what mindset is going to best facilitate goal attainment?

As Ralph Stayer wrote in *Flight of the Buffalo*, "I understand that I am the problem. Accepting that enables me to be the solution." Middle managers who align their beliefs to support their goals will enjoy more success and greater accomplishment. The high-impact management definition of success provides middle managers with a way of thinking about their jobs that is invigorating and dynamic, and that delivers results. This, coupled with beliefs that support specific goals, establishes a winning foundation for any middle manager's journey toward success.

High-impact managers pay attention to how well their definition of success is serving them. They know that there is a strong link among beliefs, actions, and results. These successful managers have learned that to improve results, beliefs that are more effective may need to be adopted while other less effective beliefs need to be discarded. High-impact management thinking is a distillation of powerful beliefs that can help busy middle managers excel and enjoy their work.

Power Partnerships

Clark was a successful and influential director of human resources (HR). His peers and other senior managers valued his input and participation. They involved Clark and his department managers in the day-to-day operations of their respective departments. Clark's HR department was effective and well respected to a degree rarely found in most organizations. Because of the fantastic partnership between Clark's staff and other departments, Clark and his team made a positive impact on the agency. However, it wasn't just a one-way street—other departments influenced Clark and his team as well.

Clark was thus a powerful role model who demonstrated how internal departments should collaborate to service one another and achieve results. Clark also reinforced this belief in collaboration when it came time to promote and evaluate his team members. Other divisions regularly sought out candidates from his department, and he frequently championed his staff for internal promotions and other positions within the organization.

What made Clark's collaborative approach even more impressive was the fact that his agency had a very competitive environment. Department leaders were more inclined to exclude, rather than include, members of internal service teams, like HR. Had it not been for the foundation of partnership that Clark had established, other department directors would not have given the HR department the same level of consideration or included its staff in as many initiatives.

Lonny could have learned a few things from Clark. Lonny thought the best way to get ahead was to flatter and try to impress senior management. He took credit for work performed by others on his team to make it appear that he was the one who had dreamed up the idea. In meetings, he was a yes man, always agreeing with higher-level managers to get their nod of approval. He applied for two promotions for which he was technically qualified, but he was turned down for both of them. The fact was that other managers did not feel they could trust him or that he shared their goals. They feared that his personal drive for self-promotion would overshadow the needs of his team and the organization.

Teamwork Drives Accomplishment

Everyone wants recognition and validation. Evening news programs love to feature stories of heroes who save the day. In the work world, however, the best and most effective way to achieve results is through teamwork—especially at the middle management level. A group of talented people rallying behind a single cause creates more success than a lone individual going off on his or her own. Middle managers who are good at collaborating are significantly more successful than those who try to go it alone. Clark understood this and was successful. Lonny did not and suffered the consequences professionally.

Developing and maintaining productive partnerships is an important skill for any manager—but most particularly for the high-impact manager. Why? Because unlike senior executives who give directives, middle managers, more often than not, do not have unilateral decision-making authority. Effective partnerships are a middle manager's currency for getting the work done.

In most organizations, departments are interdependent. When things go well, it is rarely because of a single department. It takes many teams, firing on all cylinders, to produce the best results. Middle managers can facilitate their teams' success by working together. By collaborating to improve the performance levels of other teams, middle managers can improve the productivity of their own area.

Middle managers need the cooperation and support of their peers when opportunity knocks or problems occur. Middle managers who take the time to gain peer support for new ideas and initiatives will find that implementation is easier and more trouble free. Effective high-impact managers know that their peers are a rich source of ideas and new approaches.

Partners also warn each other about emerging problems and lend a hand to avert a crisis. Communication happens on many levels in most organizations. Some topics are reviewed and discussed in staff meetings. Other information gets sent to employees via email. Sanitized and spun messages are presented to the public. Then there is the dialogue that occurs during informal conversations and lunchtime chats. This last type of information, the informal and unwritten communication, is very important. Emerging concerns, pending decisions, potentially troublesome rumors, and fresh new ideas are most likely to be heard in these outlets first. The back channel is often the most important channel in which to participate.

To ensure they are part of this communication pipeline, middle managers need to develop and maintain excellent relationships with their peers and managers. Working well with other managers also makes their work more meaningful and satisfying. When the members of a management team works together, the pace of work quickens and the energy is more positive and oriented toward success. Even when faced with significant challenges, a strong and collaborative management team can make the challenge about finding a creative solution and not about the "problem."

The Traits of Partnership

Effective partnership helps organizations deal with tough challenges and times of growth and opportunity. Every organization and department can benefit from the coordinated efforts of their talented managers. Partnership goes beyond cooperation to being a purposeful act of inclusion, collaboration, and comanagement. Merely being helpful when solicited or asked does not make one an effective partner. Partners seek each other out and proactively involve each other in day-to-day management conversations and decisions. Effective partnership emerges from a combination of several traits:

- shared purpose
- shared ownership
- mutual trust
- critical thinking
- shared success and failure
- effective inclusion and communication.

Let's look at each one.

Shared Purpose

Partners, by definition, are linked to one another. In the world of work, partners need to have a sense that they are striving for the same goal. When middle managers have a shared goal, their work together has purpose and meaning. A common target provides a foundation for partnership. Their opinions and perspectives may differ significantly, but if they are all reaching for the same goal, they can find common ground. To create a shared purpose, spend time with other middle managers learning about and discussing one another's goals and challenges.

Shared Ownership

When two or more managers share ownership of a result or outcome, they are more likely to work together effectively. Co-owning an outcome takes partnership a step beyond cooperation to collaboration. Senior managers who instill a sense of shared ownership among their middle managers will find that this expectation helps drive middle managers to partner with peers, other departments, and community members more often and more effectively. You should have periodic conversations with your peers to clarify roles and expectations in areas of shared ownership. Maintaining an open and positive dialogue will help both of you ensure that your respective areas are optimally managed to produce results.

Mutual Trust

Middle managers who trust one another will partner together more effectively. Mutual trust facilitates openness, creativity, and communication. Managers do not need to agree or see things identically to develop trusting and respectful relationships with one another. Often, an appreciation of diverse thoughts and ideas improves the regard managers have for one another. Middle managers who collaborate well almost always share mutual trust for one another. This trust is built through the process of active and healthy collaboration and comanagement. By practicing the high-impact power partnership techniques that are given in the next section, middle managers can begin to build a history together that will enhance trust and openness.

Critical Thinking

Without critical thinking, partnership is just small talk. The essence of collaboration is the act of solving problems and generating new ideas together. This work occurs best when all parties are mentally stimulated, productive, and encouraged to think critically. Results are built on the mental capabilities of middle managers working together. High-impact managers engage their peers in provocative and useful dialogue. They ask open-ended questions and seek ideas for addressing work problems.

Shared Success and Failure

Middle managers build stronger partnerships when they share the experiences of winning and losing. There is nothing like seeing a project through to completion as a team. If the project is a success, celebrating together reinforces the positive aspects of collaboration. When failures occur, middle managers should huddle together to turn the loss into a win. Sharing successes and failures brings the cycle of partnership full circle.

Effective Inclusion and Communication

Partners talk with each other often and take the initiative to include each other in formative planning and brainstorming conversations. Just as the middle manager should feel a sense of responsibility about communicating effectively with his or her employees, he or she should also expect to keep fellow middle managers in the loop.

Summing Up

The traits of partnership outlined above describe what peer-to-peer collaboration looks like in action. How do you know if you have been a good partner? You can ask a trusted friend or colleague, although the answer will generally be more favorable than objective. You can also ask your manager. But, again, managers may find it difficult to share their concerns and criticisms openly. A better strategy is to read organizational clues. Middle managers should observe how other managers interact with one another and compare this with their own experience. Middle managers can also gauge the type of partner they have been by looking at informal communication practices. How often do your peers stop by and ask for input? How open and lively are your conversations with colleagues? Look for examples of successes and failures that illustrate good or poor partnership practices. By asking questions of your peers, managers, and coworkers and then watching how they respond and interact, you can begin to glean insight into the type of partner you have been.

High-Impact Management Power Partnership Techniques

High-impact managers have learned what it takes to be a great partner. They know that the benefits of effective collaboration far outweigh the time and effort expended in creating the partnership. High-impact managers also know that good partnerships do not simply happen. There are eight techniques that they must practice and cultivate to increase the benefits of peer-to-peer collaboration. Let's look at each one.

Technique 1: Resist the Need to Control

If you have a constant need to control situations, people, or conversations, it will undermine effective collaboration with your peer group. Partnering is a give-and-take process in which no one gets to play boss. Listen and watch for both verbal and nonverbal clues that suggest other people are feeling pressured or pushed. One of the best ways to give up control in a conversation is to ask more open-ended questions and make fewer opinionated statements.

Technique 2: Spend Time with Peers

Management is a social act. The more time that middle managers spend working with one another, the easier and more natural the partnering process will feel. In addition, peers that get together often feel more comfortable asking for input, help, and participation than do those who avoid each other. Middle managers who engage peers only when necessary will receive a cooler and less helpful response. Great middle managers, both extroverts and introverts, know the value of cultivating and building relationships. You need to build relationships—relationship capital—before you need it.

Technique 3: Resolve Any Past Partnership Failures

Old conflicts and arguments affect how people relate to one another in the present and future. You need to take the initiative to resolve any prior relationship issues so as to pave the way for better and more productive collaboration in the future. The benefits of working through and getting past prior problems with other managers will more than make up for the initial discomfort of broaching the topic with them. Managers who resolve their differences will also feel less work-related stress.

If you are faced with a peer who does not seem willing to improve the relationship, you can do one of three things. First, you might try a different approach. Can you look at the situation from his or her perspective? Have you isolated the key issues or problems? It may be that what you thought was the problem is not what is actually bothering this person. Second, you are the only person you can control. Even if your peer is hanging onto a grudge, make sure that you continue to act and relate in a manner that is professional and collaborative. If you continue to take the high road, he or she might come around in time. Your third option, and the most dramatic, is to work with other peers whenever possible. You may still need to conduct business with this person, but when given the choice, it is most productive to work with those who reciprocate.

Technique 4: Communicate on Behalf of Your Peers

Effective communication is one of the most reliable predictors of a healthy partnership. Managers who keep one another in the loop and represent one another well in meetings and other conversations are generally great partners. Communicating with peers should be a regular part of your day. In addition to communicating well with one another, it is important for peers to communicate well on one another's behalf.

High-impact managers are willing and able to represent their peer's interests and needs when that person is not present in staff meetings, brainstorming sessions, and informal conversations. You may need to defend a peer's budget choices, or remind others of his or her projects that will require resources, or, more commonly, represent his or her opinions and concerns. Great partners do this even when they do not agree with their peer's point of view. When representing your middle manager peers in a positive light, you communicate that respect and care for colleagues is a key organizational value.

Technique 5: If You Cannot Say Anything Nice, Do Not Say Anything at All

Do not bad-mouth peers in front of others. It never pays to talk badly about peers, and it will burn bridges that you will need later on. Speak respectfully about other managers, even if you think ill of them. Managers who talk about other people behind their backs end up looking bad themselves. It is immature, unprofessional, and destructive to bad-mouth peers (or anyone). The saying "What goes around, comes around" certainly applies to workplace relationships. This is not to say that disagreements with peers should be ignored. The best way to deal with a difference of opinion or disagreement is to communicate it directly, in a productive way, to the person involved.

Technique 6: Take Ownership of Problems and Challenges

Don't pass the buck. Few situations can put a damper on a partnership faster than being hung out to dry by a peer. Catherine learned this the hard way. Harry blamed her for problems rooted in his department. When the president confronted Catherine about this, she was unfairly put on the defensive. Harry's choice to pass blame and abdicate his involvement in the problem diminished the partnership that he and Catherine would have in the future.

High-impact managers own problems and concerns and do not shift the blame onto other managers. If you have a complaint about how another manager is handling a situation, speak with that manager directly before taking it to the next level of management or that individual's boss. If not, you could burn bridges not only with your peer but with upper management as well. If you do need to communicate an issue to another manager, then present a fair and balanced view of the problem, including the part of it that you own.

Technique 7: Graciously Share Credit

Partners know that successes come from collaboration and that all players should share the credit. Though it may be true that one person's idea was the catalyst for the breakthrough, the overall success was a product of the joint effort. Middle managers who ensure that everyone feels a part of the success will enjoy a positive momentum going into the next project or initiative.

Technique 8: Know the Needs and Concerns of Peers, Managers, Community Members, and Employees

Middle managers will find it is easier to be good partners when they understand the needs and motivations of those with whom they regularly work. They will be in a position to anticipate needs, warn of emerging problems, and share ideas with peers if they know what is important to others. As a middle manager, you should be able to answer these questions about your employees and the other managers with whom you work on a daily basis:

- What are their needs? What are their goals? What is their purpose in the organization?
- What are their interests? What are their motivations? (These are often different from their needs.)
- What are their strengths and weaknesses? What unique skills and talents do they bring to the organization?

- What are their hot buttons? What frustrates them most?
- How do they react to changes?
- What do I expect from them? What do they expect from me and my department?

Case Study

John and Barry were vice presidents reporting to the deputy mayor. They were both very talented and opinionated. When they were together in meetings, their demeanor toward one another was either cool and aloof or confrontational. The real problem, however, came when they were not together. Both John and Barry took cheap shots at each other's expense in front of others. They also did not involve each other in decisions as often as they should have, preferring to avoid one another when possible. Barry was particularly critical and cynical of John and many of his group members. Neither was an inexperienced middle manager; they should have known better than to relate in this dysfunctional way. However, even managers with decades of experience let their opinions and emotions get the best of them.

As if the poor relations between John and Barry were not enough, the managers who reported to John and Barry were beginning to emulate the dysfunction between them. It took having a manager who worked for John and worked closely with Barry to call their attention to what was going on. To their credit, once they saw the impact their poor relationship was having on their results and their teams, they were able to become effective partners. In just a couple months, the improvement was significant, and both were realizing benefits in terms of productivity and worker satisfaction.

Summing Up

Middle managers who practice the eight partnering techniques outlined above will see immediate and long-term benefits. When peers become advocates and coaches, they add value to each other's quests for results and efficiency. Being a good partner will also reflect well on you and improve your ability to be promoted and value within the organization.

Effective partnerships are valuable assets for managers. Developing and maintaining productive relationships with peers, managers, and team members allows high-impact managers to extend their reach into the organization and improve their effectiveness. Great partners share ownership for projects, and they work together collectively to enjoy success and recover from failure. Power partnership techniques—such as spending more time with peers, resolving relationship issues, and representing others well—can help middle managers improve peer relationships.

The Reality Check: Measuring Current Performance

U ntil his last day of work, Tom would have guessed that his performance was meeting the expectations of his manager. Unfortunately, he was dead wrong, and he should have known better. Tom was a poor manager, and his boss felt that Tom and his team did not produce satisfactory work. Tom was not an effective communicator, and others felt he was untrustworthy. His manager had asked for changes that he neither implemented nor delegated to his team—even though he had told his manager he would. Several conversations occurred between Tom and his manager and his performance reviews documented Tom's deficiencies, but Tom was never able to grasp where things stood or how his manager viewed his performance.

When people in the home office spoke about Tom's colleague, Ron, their eyes would roll and they would exchange a familiar look of, "Oh, that guy." Senior managers felt that Ron was a marginal manager, someone they would replace if they could find a better alternative. Unfortunately, he had specialized technical skills that made him hard to replace. Ron openly disparaged the agency, as well as its policies and procedures. He seemed to take pride in being disrespectful and insubordinate in front of his employees. In addition, his lack of professionalism and negative demeanor rubbed off on others. A highly respected manager became a marginally performing employee after working only a few short months under Ron's supervision. Turnover on Ron's team was high. What was perhaps most unbelievable was the fact that even though he was open and brash with his opinions and criticisms, Ron had no idea that the senior management team held him in such low regard.

Jane, however, preferred to see the bright side of every story. Her glass was always half full. Though this perspective served her well in many situations, when it came to her job, her Pollyanna take on things became her undoing. She managed a department that produced several major projects each year, but she could not get the work done on time or in an organized fashion. Her manager had several specific conversations with her about areas where she needed to improve, but she did not internalize the feedback and correct her performance. She chose, instead, to believe that as long as she worked hard, everything would be fine. "I'm doing the best I can," became a frequent response when her manager asked questions about late projects. She was in denial.

Unlike Tom, Ron, or Jane, Bob was smart, creative, and a great asset to the agency. Yet he had no idea that several senior managers thought he was one of the more important managers on the team. He knew that he was doing OK but did not feel the level of satisfaction and acknowledgment equal to his managers' opinion of his performance. When times were tough and the organization needed to reduce staff, he worried that he would be first on the list of expendable managers. In reality, he was on the list of managers who were too important to let go.

Tom, Ron, Jane, and Bob all suffered from a poor or inaccurate definition of how their managers and the organization viewed their performance. Unfortunately, this is a common problem that gets in the way of a middle manager's ability to be successful. The reason this was the case may be obvious with Tom, Ron, and Jane, because their performance was unsatisfactory and their careers were in jeopardy. But Bob's inaccurate perception about his performance also affected his success, even though he underestimated his value and worth to the organization.

When you, as a middle manager, are unaware of or unclear about your current performance levels, it is difficult for you to set appropriate goals and targets. Efforts to improve need to begin with a benchmark and need to include a plan for transitioning from today's reality to tomorrow's goal. You can best improve results when you understand

- how your manager would evaluate your performance
- your reputation among managers, employees, and peers
- how well your teams are meeting goals and producing results
- how others would describe your teams' contributions and effectiveness.

Most middle managers do not have an understanding of all these areas because open, candid, and helpful feedback is not the norm in most organizations—and especially some public agencies. This is a shame, because knowledge about current performance is instrumental to most plans for change and improvement. Many efforts at change fail because they do not consider and incorporate today's realities. Ignorance is definitely not bliss when it comes to managing people, projects, and processes.

For middle managers to produce the best results possible, when making all goals and plans, they need to recognize and consider current levels of performance. It is critical that you know how your superiors, peers, and employees view your performance. If you have established the right benchmark, or starting point, improvement plans will be more realistic and operational.

The reality check is a set of techniques that you can use to understand your own performance level and the current effectiveness of your team. These techniques include methods for

- assessing your reputation within the organization
- assessing your team's reputation within the organization
- measuring your team's performance against goals and results
- communicating current performance findings to your managers and team members.

High-impact managers have a strong self-awareness and know how to keep their ears to the ground to listen for valuable information about how they and their teams are doing. The journey from good to great, or great to greater, is paved with well-planned initiatives and improvement efforts. High-impact managers have learned that successfully planned and implemented improvement initiatives start with good information.

How to Assess Your Reputation within the Organization

Middle managers must understand the reputation they have in their organization, whether it is positive or not as good as they would like. Peers, managers, and team members respond differently to each middle manager based on past results and how that manager has reacted in good times and bad. The quality of his or her relationships plays a big part in determining a manager's reputation. Middle managers with poor reputations will find it harder to garner support for initiatives and will likely not receive full and helpful collaborative efforts from others.

When people say that a manager has a good reputation, they are saying that he or she

- Can be trusted—managers are perceived as trustworthy when their words and actions are consistent. Trustworthiness is also affected by a middle manager's ability to keep confidences and represent others in a positive and professional way. Being caught talking about someone behind his or her back is a quick way to become known as untrustworthy.
- Does what he or she promises—keeping promises means doing what was agreed to, whether the agreement was spoken, written, or implied. Fulfilling implied agreements is just as important as keeping promises etched in stone or email. Middle managers who follow through on the commitments they make have integrity and will enjoy greater respect than managers who routinely do not deliver on their commitments.
- Produces good results—middle managers who pull their weight and add value to the organization are respected and appreciated. Delivering results is a fundamental requirement for all middle managers. Managers who produce poor results will not be well regarded by other managers or peers because they are not doing their part to contribute to agency success. The exception to this is if the results are lacking due to conditions not under the middle manager's control.

- Is a pleasure or easy to work with—those managers with whom other staff members like to work will be perceived more favorably than those who are less fun and amiable. It is not important that a manager be an extrovert for him or her to be considered a pleasure to work with. Managers of all styles and philosophical persuasions can be easy to work with as long as they are accessible, interested, and helpful.
- Is knowledgeable and creative in their chosen field—managers and peers acknowledge and appreciate middle managers who know their stuff; this includes technical or specialized skills related to the department they manage. Furthermore, others in the organization will think well of middle managers who continue to learn and grow.
- Is an asset to the organization—in most organizations, only a small percentage of managers are outstanding assets. When senior management considers a middle manager to be a great asset, he or she has demonstrated the ability and desire to contribute to the organization in a variety of ways. He or she will tend to be a manager who could successfully manage most departments or projects.

When people say that a manager has a bad reputation, they are saying that he or she

- Can't be trusted—perhaps he or she has abused confidences or burned someone in the past.
- Does not follow through on commitments—he or she has let people down.
- Does not get the job done when others do—his or her results are disappointing.
- Is in some way difficult to work with—he or she is not a team player.
- Does not have the right skills or aptitude—he or she lacks creativity or technical expertise.
- Is not an important contributor—he or she does not make a difference.

You probably will find it difficult and uncomfortable to take the steps necessary to learn about the reputation you have established in your organization. However, it would be even more undesirable to have no idea how others perceive you.

Middle managers can use three possible approaches to discover their reputation. The first, and easiest, approach is to ask. This method will work in environments where honest and open feedback is available.

Middle managers should also try the second approach, which is observation, particularly if the first approach does not yield full or truthful information. Many peers, managers, and team members will not feel comfortable being candid about their thoughts.

If the first two approaches fail to provide you with the necessary information, then try the third approach, which is to use an objective third party. Managers who need to use the third approach will often have a reputation that makes people reluctant and guarded with their feedback. In addition, middle managers in higher-level positions receive less honest feedback than their colleagues at lower levels do. Some people will be reluctant, for example, to tell a department head about areas in which he or she needs to improve. Middle managers should be aware that it is going to be harder to get useful and helpful feedback as they progress up the career ladder in their organization. This is unfortunate, because everyone needs good feedback to perform at his or her best.

Let's look more closely at each of these three approaches.

Approach 1: Ask

An effective way for you to determine your reputation is to ask peers, managers, and team members. This, of course, works best if you have trusting and collaborative relationships that allow for open and honest communication. The questions that you ask and how you ask them are also important.

You may choose to meet with people one-to-one, but this approach is only going to yield accurate results in the most open and trusting work environments.

A sample form you can use to solicit feedback can be downloaded for free at www.lisahaneberg.com on the My Books page. Ask your peers, managers, and team members to fill out this form and return it to you. You can choose to have the form returned directly to you, or to another person if you think this will help people be more open and honest. Ask for a response within five days and encourage respondents to be open and honest. Compile the responses. Notice the trends and the relative rankings. Though respondents may not feel comfortable answering questions in a derogatory manner, the ranking and ratings will reveal which of the managerial traits are of the most concern. For example, if a manager is not reliable, chances are good that respondents will rank this trait toward the bottom, or 7, in most of the returned forms. The completed survey, shown in example 4-1, represents real feedback given to a middle manager. The scores have all been averaged.

The overall interpretation of the feedback from this survey that this particular manager should arrive at is that she is very well regarded and respected by the folks who participated. This group sees her as an extremely results-oriented and highly productive manager. These are very positive scores. However, even with positive scores such as these, there will likely be one or two areas in which you need to improve. This middle manager's results are no exception.

First, it is clear that developing relationships is a relative weakness for this manager and may even be a potential future derailing factor. Related to this is her tendency to judge others and come across as too blunt and direct. These criticisms are all related to how this middle manager works with others. It is also apparent that she needs to be more cognizant of how she comes across to others and how she talks about other people.

It is likely that this middle manager has been battling these weaknesses for a long time. Without this feedback, it is likely that these problem areas could become more severe and begin affecting her career. It is also quite interesting that this middle manager scored no points in part 3 of example 4-1 under the option "can get emotional." Though this means that she keeps her cool, it also relates to her tendency to lack empathy and be too matter-of-fact.

As these results show, even very strong and well-respected middle managers will benefit from learning more about the reputation they have

Example 4-1. Middle Management Survey for: Mr./Ms. Middle Manager

Please answer the survey openly and honestly. I am interested in learning the good, the bad, and the ugly. I consider this tool to be a part of my overall development plan and value your feedback. Please return the completed survey to me by next Monday. Thank you!

Part 1: Middle Management Qualities and Traits

For each trait listed, indicate whether this particular trait is a strength of mine or a weakness, or somewhere in the middle. If a weakness, please do not hesitate to point this out. Please also rank these traits from 1–7, 1 being the trait I am strongest in and 7 the trait that is the greatest weakness for me.

Middle Management Quality/Trait	Strength	Average	Weakness	Rank
Timely in regard to work and projects	xxxxxx			4.25
Reliable	xxxxxx			3.75
Easy to work with, even when times are difficult	xxxxx	x		4.5
Acts quickly and follows up	xxxxxx			3.25
Results oriented	xxxxxx			1.25
Skilled manager	xxxxx	x		3.5
Builds and maintains relationships	x	xxxxx		6.75

Part 2: Open-Ended Questions

Complete the following questions, providing as many specifics as possible.

Share a time when this manager let someone down at work. *Too quick to pass judgment. Cannot think of a time. Only minor things (4).*

Share the most important contribution this manager has made to the organization in the last year. *Department workflow. Developing good processes. Elevated the level of her department (3).*

What has been his or her greatest failure in the last year? *Don't know. Qualities of all her employees not up to standard (3).*

How well do you believe this manager represents you and your interests? *Very well. Always honest. Always supportive. For the most part excellent but there may also be times when she gives an opinion about me that is inaccurate and is not helpful.*

Do you consider this manager highly productive, satisfactorily productive, or below average in productivity? *Highly productive (5).*

What do people like most and least about working with this manager?

Most: *Knows her stuff. Is always there for you. Thoroughness and dependability. Smart, quick, funny. Gets things done. Keeps people focused and honest.*

Least: *Can be very matter-of-fact, lacking empathy. Afraid you may not measure up in her eyes. Bluntness. Sometimes abrupt and too direct.*

Part 3: Descriptive Phrases

Each section below contains four phrases. Spread 100 points across the four phrases, giving more points to those phrases that are more descriptive of this manager and his or her performance and fewer points to those phrases that are less descriptive. You can, for example, give 50 points to the first two phrases and 0 points to the other two, or give 30 points to one while giving the others, 20, 10, and 40 points, respectively.

Management style:	100 Points Total
Teamwork oriented	31
Values individual initiative and creativity	31
Values security and predictability	11
Hard-driving competitiveness and focus on results	27
This manager is thought to be:	100 Points Total
Trustworthy	28
Reliable	26
A good partner	22
Responsible	24
When times get tough/busy, this manager:	100 Points Total
Plans well and is organized	56
Can get emotional	0
Represents the needs of his or her team members well	44
Can get overwhelmed	0

developed in the organization. Paying attention to relative rankings and reoccurring themes will help you to better understand your strengths and weaknesses.

Approach 2: Observe

Another way that managers can determine their reputation is to observe how others interact with and around them. Peers, managers, and team members communicate and respond in ways that reflect their feelings. Managers should take note of these aspects:

- Inclusivity versus exclusivity—managers held in high regard will find themselves invited to participate in more conversations and meetings to discuss emerging issues than middle managers who do not enjoy as positive a reputation.
- Project assignments—highly regarded managers will find that senior managers ask them to lead or take part in important projects.
- Confidential information—all middle managers are privy to some proprietary information. There are many conversations, however, that take place about new ideas, potential deals, and upcoming changes in the organization. Managers learn who does not keep confidences or likes to spread gossip. If you find yourself excluded from sensitive information, your reputation may be suffering.
- What happens in tough situations—results-oriented managers will be the logical go-to people when something needs to be done quickly and well. Managers who have failed to meet deadlines or produce results in the past will not be on the top of the list of folks to go to when opportunity or problems strike.
- Confidence in goals and deadlines—managers known for delivering on their goals and deadlines will find that others have confidence in their work and plans.
- Collaboration and cooperation from peers—peers and managers will treat managers who have been great partners more warmly and collaboratively than they do those who have not been good partners. Peers are also more likely to look out for those with whom they have established a positive and strong reputation.

- Career progression—managers can get an indication about their reputation by looking at how their career has progressed. This includes the promotions they have received as well as those that they wanted but did not receive. Managers who fail to receive promotions should assume there is probably something about their reputations that needs improvement.

- Feedback and performance evaluations—managers should notice what their manager does and does not say when providing feedback or explaining a performance evaluation. Which skills or responsibilities does the manager, without hesitation, say are the manager's strengths? Which responsibilities does the manager talk about using qualifiers or less favorable terms?

Managers who notice how others treat them should be able to get a feel for the reputations they have within the organization. One caution: Inclusion and participation based on a person's job or functional expertise are also required. The finance director must provide input on finances, the geologist will take part in projects involving landslides, and the captain needs to answer questions about navigation. When evaluating reputation, it is important to separate interactions and inclusion initiated because of one's position from other situations. Senior managers ask their valued middle managers to join in a wide variety of discussions and projects and include them early on when problems arise.

Approach 3: Use a Facilitator or Third Party

If you do not want to use approaches 1 and 2, or have tried them without success, you might want to enlist help from an objective third party. In many organizations, this is a regular and normal practice. Some organizations have a corporate psychologist on staff or executive coaches who help senior and middle managers discover and improve their reputations. Other organizations use human resources generalists or management development trainers to meet this need. Depending on the situation, an objective third party can use surveys, interviews, and observation to help you determine how to improve your effectiveness.

Another objective method that many organizations use is 360-degree feedback instruments. These surveys are often chosen because they collect and compare information from the person (a self-assessment) as well as from his or her manager(s), peers, and employees. Most 360-degree feedback instruments have questions that measure the middle manager's reputation. These feedback instruments, however, are only as good as the data that go into them and the follow-up that results from them. They are most useful if you can get several peers, team members, and managers to complete the surveys and then positively and proactively respond to the feedback you receive.

Managers interested in learning what their reputations are in an organization can use any of these approaches. Great managers do what others don't or won't. Many managers never bother to think about how others see them or if they have a derailing factor getting in the way of their success. Middle managers who take the time and expend the energy to discover their reputations will experience, at the very least, an "aha moment" and, at best, a breakthrough. High-impact managers know their strengths and weaknesses and use this knowledge to grow and improve.

Case Study

Art had applied for two promotions and received neither. One was an internal support position in which he would interact with many other departments. When managers from other departments found out that Art had applied for this promotion, several expressed their concerns. They didn't want to work with him. Though he was highly qualified, he did not have the most important qualification: demonstrated ability and experience developing and maintaining positive work relationships. The hiring manager told him the truth. He was not going to get the position because he had a reputation for being difficult to work with and had burned bridges with internal customers over the last year. Until he fixed these problems, his career would go nowhere.

When faced with a significant derailing factor that affects their careers, many managers crumble. High-impact managers, however, use this situation as an opportunity to create a new definition of success. They look at what can be improved because they realize that success and accolades will naturally follow as a result of their being an outstanding partner with whom to work. Many managers find that they can repair burned bridges and reestablish credibility by consistently being collaborative and productive. It can be hard to deal with harsh feedback, but not doing so can permanently derail your career.

How to Assess Your Team's Reputation within the Organization

The purchasing team within the city was well regarded and enjoyed high levels of participation in many of the agency's major initiatives. Many departments viewed working with purchasing as a positive and worthwhile activity and felt that the purchasing team helped them manage their part of the organization more effectively. Members of purchasing were proud of their accomplishments and took their role of supporting the organization seriously. The managers of other departments coveted these team members for open positions, and most team members experienced positive career moves every few years.

In contrast, the accounting department was known as being inflexible, inaccurate, and slow. Managers did not trust the numbers it produced and felt they had to clean up after its errors. The processes the accounting department's team members used and the way they conducted business made it more difficult for managers to manage their departments. Many individuals on the accounting team did not progress or receive promotions. Of the talented employees who joined the accounting team, many applied for a transfer within a year. The employees who stayed on the team were marginal performers. The situation was so bad that people in other departments often circumvented processes to avoid contact with the accounting department.

These two examples may seem extreme, but both are real and commonplace. Most middle managers would like to see their team regarded similarly to the purchasing team in this example and not like the accounting team. By taking the time to evaluate your team's reputation, you will have the information and starting point you need to begin the improvement process. All teams have the potential to be well regarded high performers. Making sure that your team is making a positive contribution to the organization should be your top priority, because it will drive success, satisfaction, and results. To discover and define your team's reputation in the organization, you should

■ Ask peers and managers.
■ Observe and listen.
■ Measure performance.
■ Talk with team members.

Let's look more closely at each of these techniques.

Ask Peers and Managers

To assess the reputation of your team, you can ask many of the same questions you would use to determine your own reputation. For individuals and teams alike, reputations form around and center on similar questions: Can they be trusted? Do they deliver results? Are they positive to work with? Are they reliable? Are they responsive? To understand the answers to these questions, middle managers should regularly talk with their peers and managers, asking open-ended questions like these:

■ In what ways does this department excel?
■ In what ways does this department fail to meet expectations?
■ If you were the manager, what improvements or changes would you make to this team?
■ What is it like to work with this team?
■ When was the last time you felt frustrated because of this team's performance or an interaction with team members?
■ What is one change that would make working with this team more pleasurable?
■ What goal or improvement initiative would be most worthwhile over the next year?
■ What do others say about this team?

When a middle manager talks with his or her peers and manager about how to improve the team's performance, he or she will often get valuable information about how they currently regard the team. Discovering a team's reputation is not nearly as hard as determining one's own reputation.

Observe and Listen

Middle managers can also pick up information about their team's reputation by paying attention to verbal and nonverbal clues. In meetings, how do people refer to the team? When project managers assign tasks for a cross-functional project, is the team included begrudgingly or enthusiastically as an important contributor? Do people try to include team members or go around them to get their work done? It is common practice to see alternative systems and processes pop up for the sole purpose of not having to involve your particular department or team? If this happens, it should be a giant clue that your team suffers from a poor reputation. For example, with the accounting team mentioned above, several departments tracked their own data and created their own reports. A couple of departments found ways around the invoicing system to ensure valued vendors were paid on time. Middle managers who make it a point to observe these activities can be more proactive in preventing needless duplications of work and improving their team's performance and reputation.

Measure Performance

Teams that meet their goals and produce results will often also have a positive reputation in the organization. Middle managers should know how their team is performing for many reasons, including understanding if the agency sees the team as a positive contributor. The next section offers techniques for measuring team performance.

Talk with Team Members

Most team members know and sense how others in the organization regard their team. If the team is enjoying a positive reputation, its members will feel pride and satisfaction. If the team has a poor reputation, this will likely be a source of stress and frustration for its members. For middle managers, there are two significant advantages to asking the team's members about its reputation. First, managers will learn valuable and useful information that they can use to set goals and select improvement initiatives. Second, team members who talk about their performance are more likely to become part of the solution and improvement effort. And along with asking your team members' opinions, try to solicit their input and ideas for getting to the next level of performance and effectiveness.

How to Measure Your Team's Performance against Goals and Results

Along with understanding your team's reputation, you also need to measure its performance to establish the correct goals. This goes beyond knowing that everyone is working hard and doing their best to taking the time to measure throughput and results.

Often, a team is producing much more than the manager or the organization realizes. Sometimes the reverse is also true. Clearly defining current performance helps establish the starting point for all goals and initiatives. Many managers think of measuring performance as an undesirable and a low-value-added task. How mistaken these managers are! Team performance measures help middle managers gain the support and resources they need and make their jobs easier and more fruitful, as shown in the case study about Tim.

Case Study

Tim's predecessors had requested additional personnel to process the massive amounts of information that flowed through his department. But senior managers had turned down their requests and, in some cases, cut their resources. Tim could see the need for people to process the information more effectively and quickly, and he knew that he would need senior managers' support to dedicate resources in this area. He did something the managers before him had not: He measured performance and productivity. He determined that each employee spent more than 35 percent of his or her time on processing, and, that as a team, their efficiency was lower than desired. By dedicating personnel to the sole task of processing, efficiencies would improve and overall personnel costs would decrease. Had Tim not measured current performance and produced the data to back up his assertions, it is unlikely that he would have found support for creating new positions.

High-impact managers make it a priority to know and continually measure their team's performance. They do so by establishing ongoing systems and practices for updating and communicating throughput and results. They know the key financial and nonfinancial metrics that matter most. To determine the correct things to measure, ask yourself these questions:

1. What is the most important contribution that internal and external customers expect this team to make? Is the team meeting the expectations of internal and external customers?
2. What are the primary products and services produced by this team? What are the team's productivity and throughput related to these products and services?
3. Is the team meeting its goals? Why or why not?
4. How would this team's internal and external customers define the responsiveness and speed that they expect from this team? Is the team meeting expectations?
5. What major initiatives or projects is this team supporting? Are team members completing their project work on time and well?
6. What expectations exist about improving departmental processes and methods? Are team members taking the time and using initiative to improve how they do their work?

On the basis of the answers to these questions, you can begin to identify the most important metrics to track. It is helpful to create a quick reference sheet of several metrics, so that you can regularly review them with your team members and managers (a tool for communicating metrics, called the "High-Impact Management Playbook," is presented in chapter 5). Furthermore, middle managers who involve the team in measuring and reporting on these metrics will improve their team members' connection, empowerment, and ownership of the department's results and success.

Case Study

Each year during the budgeting process, senior managers challenged Corky to lower the human resources (HR) department's head count. This was always a frustrating process because she knew that, if anything, she needed more help. Although the agency was small, it hired and then laid off many seasonal employees each year. Corky measured the throughput and results of the HR team. The numbers were enlightening and helpful. The department was recruiting, hiring, processing, evaluating, and terminating employees at a rate more typical of a company four times its size. The usual ratio of one HR person for every 100 employees would not work for this department. Corky did need more help and, with good information and measurements, she was able to get it.

How to Communicate Current Performance Findings to Managers and Team Members

Some middle managers take the time to measure performance but then fail to communicate performance to their team members or their managers. Management is a social act. If you collect information but then do nothing with it, you are not truly managing. Measurements can only be useful when managers and team members discuss, respond to, and use measurement information to improve performance in the future. To communicate current performance, middle managers should

- Meet regularly with their managers to review performance—at this meeting, you should come prepared with a list of current performance measures, a summary of those things that are going well, concerns, and your action plan for addressing the concerns. This meeting can be brief, as short as 30 minutes. Middle managers should meet with their managers on at least a monthly basis. During peak production periods or major initiatives, meetings should occur more often.
- Discuss team performance and metrics at every team meeting—ask open-ended questions to clarify concerns or to collect team members' ideas for resolving issues regarding throughput or results. Speak about concerns and performance shortfalls in a matter-of-fact way that communicates to team members that performance needs to improve but that this is not something personal.
- Post team measurements in a visible way—ensure the team updates key performance measures regularly. Each team should

have three to five fundamental deliverables that are most important. For example, the human resource team might track hiring accuracy and short-term turnover.

- Use information about current performance levels when planning future initiatives or setting goals—projects and initiatives will be more successful if the team's strengths and weaknesses are accounted for and considered in their planning.
- Be sure to celebrate excellent team performance, major milestones, and accomplishments—share these important performance achievements with peers and the rest of the organization.

Communicating current team performance enables managers and team members to react and begin the process of celebration or improvement. Most middle managers do not talk about team performance enough with their teams or managers. The many rewards of regular and open conversations about metrics include higher manager confidence, higher team morale, and better results.

When you understand the reputation you have in an organization, the reputation of your team, and their current performance metrics, you arm yourself with powerful information that will aid in planning, goal setting, and improvement initiatives. High-impact managers perform a reality check by practicing habits and employing methods that ensure they are aware of their work environment. In time, these habits and methods will become second nature and a normal part of your middle management practices.

Using the High-Impact Management Playbook to Facilitate Peak Performance

In sports, the goals are clear. Well-conceived and clearly communicated plays determine what each player does. Objectives are clarified during practice sessions, and each team member's performance is reviewed in detail after each game. Every player knows his or her stats and those of the team. Skill and results determine each team member's position and play time. Like great coaches, high-impact managers use planning, measurement, and communication skills to create performance targets and improve team accountability, execution, and results.

Just as a sports team uses a playbook to develop strategy and refine its game plan, so too can high-impact managers use a similar tool to refine their management practices and facilitate attaining peak performance from themselves and their team. Using the High-Impact Management Playbook will enable you to set goals, establish plans, and measure performance in less time than with more conventional methods. The result will be significant improvements in work completion, quality, and throughput.

The Playbook

In sports, teams need to respond quickly and plan well between each game. They do not have time for elaborate processes or cumbersome tracking mechanisms. The High-Impact Management Playbook (see figure 5-1) uses the efficient and time-saving aspects of the playbooks used in sports and adds features that meet the needs of busy middle managers. (The playbook can be downloaded at www.lisahaneberg.com.)

Elements of a typical sports playbook include

- the strategy for each game
- a list of regular plays organized by category
- strategies for communicating and exchanging plays with others
- detailed statistics on each player and the players on the opponent's team
- the strengths and weaknesses of the team and its opponents.

The High-Impact Management Playbook contains measures, indicators, and lists that many agencies track and value. It is important that you use this playbook only as a starting point. The playbook will be most useful when you customize it to meet your specific needs. Its elements include

- descriptions of priorities and approaching projects
- short-term and long-term goals
- detailed metrics on the key financial and nonfinancial measures for the team
- ongoing work productivity statistics
- space for updates on work projects or tasks
- ways of optimizing workflow
- a list of concerns and barriers facing the team.

The playbook is an invaluable tool that will help you focus your time and energy on the tasks that will have the greatest impact on your team's results. It provides a snapshot of current team performance, priorities, and work assignments. Let's consider a detailed description of each section of the playbook shown in figure 5-1.

Priorities and Upcoming Projects

This section should include a brief list of future projects or initiatives that team members should consider and begin preparing for when planning their work. For example, if you work for an organization that experiences seasonal highs and lows, this section can be used to remind team members of important launch dates for busy times.

Figure 5-1. The High-Impact Management Playbook

Ongoing Work		Status		Key Metrics		Current Performance	Priorities and Upcoming Projects
Short-Term Goals				Long-Term Goals			
							Concerns & Barriers
Task	Owner	Deadline		Task	Owner	Deadline	
							Productivity Questions Why are we doing this? What difference will it make? Is there a better action to take? Is there an easier way? Are the right people involved? Does it improve results?

Short-Term and Long-Term Goals

Short-term goals are those your team will complete in the next one to six months. Long-term goals should mirror or support those listed in your agency's strategic plan. Well-written goals include time frames, owners of tasks, and expected results. Reviewing both short-term and long-term goals on a regular basis helps your team stay aligned and able to meet today's needs and support the organization's vision for the future. Other sections of the playbook should include tasks that support the goals listed here.

Key Financial and Nonfinancial Team Metrics

Each team should have a set of metrics that it collects, reviews, and reports periodically. These metrics measure how well the team is doing relative to the fundamental contributions its has been asked to make. For a marketing team, for example, the metrics could include customer acquisition costs, the return-on-investment (ROI) for marketing campaigns, and exposure in the marketplace. If you are not already tracking these types of data, you should start because this information will help you stay abreast of performance and enable you to notice trends and emerging problems.

Ongoing Work Productivity

Each department has ongoing work that is important to track. Often this work will consume a significant portion of your team's time and resources. Examples of this type of work include processing checks, answering customer calls, processing new employees, maintaining systems, and supporting field operations. In this section of the playbook, you should list two or three of the most important ongoing products or services and describe how the team will track productivity. The items in this section will probably not change much from week to week, but productivity will vary with time.

Work Projects and Tasks

This portion of the playbook is the most dynamic and offers the clearest and quickest benefit to middle managers. The tasks that your team needs to complete are listed, along with the deadlines and owners for each task. As your team completes tasks, you can cross out these tasks in the playbook or leave them listed to help team members communicate the status of their work. Some managers will prefer to complete one playbook each week and keep previous copies in their day planner. Others may choose to keep one master playbook.

Work Flow Optimization

Middle managers use the playbook to track work against current and emerging priorities. By reviewing the playbook often and asking yourself questions about how you are using your resources, you can ensure that your team is producing at its best. Middle managers should also recognize and plan for short periods of high or low work demands by adjusting assignments or bringing in short-term help.

Concerns and Barriers

Listing concerns and barriers is critical to keeping you and your team members focused on resolving problems that could have an impact on throughput. Throughout the day and week, the middle manager fills this section with the normal challenges of running a function. As he or she crosses each entry off the list, it is a sign that work is flowing productively again. This section, more than any other, highlights high-impact management work in action!

Communicating the Playbook

A sports team uses its playbook faithfully. It is the central tool for communicating priorities and progress to the team. Producing consistent wins takes teamwide communication and participation.

This approach is not as common in business—though it should be. During the development and launch of Black & Decker's DeWalt line, product teams met frequently to discuss status, priorities, and their game plan. They also took time to celebrate successes along the way. Sometimes the team congratulated the engineers for creating a new and better feature. Other times, the marketing folks won praise for a well-timed coup in the marketplace.

Middle managers in any industry—private or public sector—can use the High-Impact Management Playbook in the same manner. Management is a social act and the playbook is an excellent way to facilitate communication among you and your supervisors, team members, peers, and managers. The playbook is an organic tool, which should change to represent the current priorities and needs of your department. Middle managers should have their playbook with them at all meetings and review it at the beginning of each workday. Those who use a day planner for appointments should insert their playbook in their binders for easy reference. High-technology middle managers who prefer BlackBerries or laptops can load their playbook into their favorite device. By reviewing each section of the playbook at team meetings, middle managers can get input from team members on items to change or add, as well as gain understanding of and commitment to their priorities. This practice will also provide an opportunity for team members to ask questions, express concerns, identify barriers, and ask for necessary support.

How to Use the High-Impact Management Playbook

You can begin using the High-Impact Management Playbook by filling out each section and sharing it with your managers and team members to get input. If you do not currently have team metrics, you can take a few minutes to think about what they should be or hold a team meeting to discuss metrics as a group. Both long-term and short-term goals come from yearly plans. Middle managers who are not presently creating a departmental plan can use the tutorial at the end of this chapter.

Update the playbook daily, weekly, or as needed. Take it to all meetings. Information shared at meetings often fits into the upcoming projects or concerns and barriers sections. You will want to keep these and other sections current to get the most benefit from using the playbook.

Use the playbook as a platform for team update meetings. Revise and redistribute copies after each meeting so all your team members understand the plan and the action items for which they are responsible. Share the playbook with the peers who work most closely with your team. Doing so will create greater understanding, generate support, and improve relationships. The playbook is an excellent communication tool.

Middle managers can download the full-size version of the High-Impact Management Playbook at www.lisahaneberg.com on the My Books page. Finding a size and format that is easiest to use and maintain is an important part of using the playbook to track and improve performance.

Customizing the Playbook

Middle managers should customize their playbooks to suit their needs. The playbook is most useful when it captures your daily and weekly concerns. The intent of a playbook is to provide a quick reference for middle managers and their team members that, when used, helps them stay aligned and on track. Throughout the day, you should carry the playbook and update sections as needed. Examples of sections that you may want to add to the playbook include

- meetings to schedule or prepare for
- team meeting discussion topics

- phone numbers of important contacts
- questions for peers or managers
- areas needing research or analysis
- action items that you have requested from others.

By customizing your playbook, you will optimize the effectiveness and relevance of this tool and management practice. Middle managers can tailor the playbook to meet their needs and complement their preferred planning style.

Creating a Departmental Strategic Plan: A Tutorial

Depending on your organization's size and culture, you may or may not receive the training and coaching needed to create a departmental strategic plan. A departmental plan includes a departmental vision aligned with the overall agency vision; three to five objectives that support agency objectives; and goals, projects, and initiatives that produce these objectives. Each organization may use slightly different terminology, but don't worry about that. The exact names are not important. The importance of a plan is that it tells the you and your team:

- why they exist and the contribution they are expected to make to the organization
- their priorities and most important initiatives
- the plan for delivering the promised results.

To get to this point, you, as a middle manager, need to learn and understand the broader strategic plan and answer several questions about long-term and short-term needs, changes, and opportunities. The following questions can be used to help brainstorm needs and considerations for a departmental strategic plan.

Long term—one to three years:

- Based on the strategic plan (developed by senior management), what will be the purpose of this function over the next several years?
- How will the work change?

- What skills and resources will my team members need? How will these skills be developed in time to meet tomorrow's challenges?
- What changes should occur today to meet strategic goals?
- What are the major milestones to observe/strive for over the next three years?
- What's coming down the pike, and will it need attention?
- Will a different kind of management be required to produce different results? How should new skills be acquired and put into place?
- What is my department doing today that does not support the strategic direction?
- What should my team be working on to ensure that it is being aligned with future goals and initiatives?
- What do my team members need to know about the future direction?

Midterm—this year:

- What does the organization expect my team to accomplish this year? What are my team's deliverables? What are my team's current strengths and weaknesses?
- What will it take to deliver? What resources are required in the areas of people, roles, systems, processes, and projects? What should be included in the department plan and budget to achieve objectives?
- What changes will occur during the next year? Does my team have a clear implementation plan for change defined and in place?
- Does my team need to realign roles or processes to fulfill this year's department plan? Will my staff need new skills?
- What are the most important monthly and quarterly milestones? What processes are required to ensure that my department is focused on achieving these milestones?
- Are there decisions that need to be made to enable the team's success?

Short term—this month:

- What is the work plan for the month? What key results does my team need to deliver? Can they get all of the work done? How will I communicate progress on the work plan?
- What are the barriers to my team's success? What is the plan for ensuring that barriers are defined and removed?
- Which metrics provide the best information about the team's productivity and results?
- What meetings should I schedule, plan, and lead to facilitate good communication, creativity, coordination, and/or problem solving?
- How should I spend my time to make the greatest impact?
- What coaching and/or development should I seek?
- How will I ensure that others make timely decisions affecting the team?
- What is my plan for coaching and developing my staff?
- What worries my team members, managers, and peers most? With whom should I talk about these concerns? Is there anything I have been putting off?

Weekly/daily:

- What does my team need to accomplish today or this week, and what's the plan for ensuring that it all gets done?
- What are the problems and barriers getting in the way of productivity? Who should be working on these barriers? How can I remove barriers today?
- With whom do I need to communicate today?
- How should I spend my time today?
- Have I prepared for today's meetings?

These questions, though a bit overwhelming, will help you brainstorm about the type of information needed for the departmental strategic plan. Middle managers should be able to answer each question. The rough data will help you create the vision, objectives, and goals for your departmental plan. Though formats and terms differ from agency to agency, here are definitions for each part of the departmental strategic plan:

- *Vision:* The vision is a short statement, one to three sentences long, that states the main purpose for your team and the contribution it makes to the organization. Example: The PUD marketing department serves as the voice of this utility in the marketplace. Marketing creates and conveys the brands, products, and services in ways that maximize market share, revenues, and customer satisfaction. The work of the marketing department is fundamental to the agency's revenue generation and goals for program growth.

- *Objectives:* Most departments should have three to five broad targets covering each major area or function within the department. Each objective should define the target, the timeline for completion, and the measures of success. Example: Utilize the web to improve knowledge of the product, market reach, and to facilitate revenue generation. In the next year, implement two or three web-based tools or products that generate revenue at an ROI of at least 10:1 (that is, they generate $10 in revenue for every $1 spent).

- *Goals:* Most department plans contain two to five goals for each objective. Goals may be initiatives or projects. Goals must be specific, measurable, and have deadlines. Example: Develop and implement a plan for training contractors using web-based technology. Complete 40 training sessions with an average attendance of 15 persons and an average ROI of 10:1 or better by the end of the year.

After creating a rough plan, you should review the complete plan to ensure that it is realistic. Departmental plans should be challenging and represent the work that can be accomplished when the team is highly productive. It is common to see departmental plans that are not practical or possible. Middle managers who create plans that contain too many projects or initiatives are setting their teams up for failure and frustration.

If the objectives or projects are being requested by senior management, it may be necessary to negotiate the plan. Often it is a question of people and resources. Many middle managers do not even bother to stand up for their teams when they are being asked to do more than is possible. Middle managers should do any or all of the following to ensure that their plan is robust and doable:

- Challenge conventional thinking. Is the plan really impossible? What if the department were reorganized or realigned?
- Negotiate the work. Are there projects or tasks that could be discontinued to allow new and higher priority work to be completed? Be clear about what the department can and cannot do.
- Ask for more resources. Are new projects or initiatives important enough to warrant additional and dedicated resources?
- Ask the team. The team members may offer great ideas for how the work can get done. They often know of ways to save resources and reduce waste.
- Ask peers for their ideas and input. Do they think the plan is unrealistic? What would they do if this were their plan?

Once the middle manager and senior managers negotiate and agree to the plan, the middle manager should communicate it to all team members. Then the High-Impact Management Playbook picks up where the departmental plan leaves off and serves as a daily tool to enable middle managers to stay on track with their plans.

Mucky-Muck Obstructions: Navigating the Corporate Obstacle Course

Middle managers link teams, systems, and processes together to produce results. This requires working with many different people and under varied circumstances, which, in turn, can produce conflict, contradiction, and chaos—also known as mucky-muck. Mucky-muck causes a great deal of teeth-gnashing frustration, often reflected in comments such as:

- Why is it so hard to get anything done around here?
- Why did I waste my time?
- Why wasn't I told that up front?
- It takes forever to get a decision made in this organization.
- She and I just don't see eye to eye. I'll sit this one out.

Dealing with some mucky-muck is an inevitable part of any job and especially in a large government setting; however, unresolved mucky-muck can quickly turn to quicksand that mires productivity, morale, and positive communication. To be successful as a middle manager, you need to be part investigator, part mind reader, and part magician. Knowing how to navigate through mucky-muck is an essential management skill.

Sixteen Variations of Mucky-Muck

The first step in getting through the mucky-muck is to recognize what it looks like. Like various strains of a virus, all mucky-muck shares some common elements. Mucky-muck is generally rooted in people's emotional and defensive reactions to feelings of personal censure or self-doubt. Other forms of mucky-muck share an element of process, structure, or role getting in the way of common sense. Every work environment will breed and support different kinds of mucky-muck. Let's look at the 16 forms that are the most common in many organizations.

Variation 1: Miscommunication

Lou wondered why it was taking Mike so long to respond to his request for a few cost projections. He didn't know that Mike was upset because he thought that Lou was trying to usurp a portion of his project. This was, in fact, not the case; but Mike responded emotionally to the perceived threat and thus had no incentive to help Lou.

Middle managers spend a surprisingly large amount of time clearing up confusion or hurt feelings that arise from miscommunication. Emails are one of the biggest miscommunication generators because it is hard for the recipient to interpret the intent and tenor of brief, written messages. To reduce the likelihood of miscommunication, make requests clear and specific, and provide examples to illustrate your meaning. Regularly talk in person or on the phone and resist the urge to assume that you know what others are thinking. To avoid this type of mucky-muck, it is best to err on the side of overcommunicating with peers and team members.

Variation 2: Politics

Jim and his managers met with Jake to share their plan for the coming year. They knew they needed to get Jake's support before they presented their plan to the mayor. If the mayor knew that Jake supported the plan, he would be less likely to reject it. It often worked best to have Jake share the plan with the mayor one-to-one to address the mayor's concerns before the management team met with him. Although it took a few extra steps, this was the way Jim was best able to implement important changes.

The posturing and maneuvering that occur within a group or organization is its politics. Nonpolitical managers, like Jim, are often forced to play politics to get things done. Gaining, keeping, or controlling power is often the motivation for politics. Managers who are political often think in hierarchical terms and show a preference for exclusivity. Though politics is an inevitable part of most public agencies, middle managers can reduce the negative impact of politics by learning the unwritten rules about how decisions are made. It is also important to ensure that you do not let concerns about status, ego, or self-preservation get in the way of your productivity. It is best to focus on those actions that will benefit work relationships and results.

Variation 3: Passing the Buck and Pointing Fingers

Harry's boss asked him why one of his road crew teams was short several staff members and was unable to meet its productivity goals. Harry had a problem supervisor that was causing people to walk off the job with no notice; but instead of being open about this, he blamed the problem on the human resources department. Harry knew that this problem's root cause was the supervisor, and that he had neglected to do anything about it, hoping the situation would improve without his intervention.

Every day, middle managers face tough questions about their teams, processes, and results. If they suffer from low self-esteem and confidence, more often than not they will try to make sure they don't appear to be wrong or at fault in front of others. This may manifest itself in blaming their peers, managers, or, worse yet, subordinates for problems. As one can imagine, this form of mucky-muck breeds more obstacles, such as miscommunication and burned bridges. Middle managers who encounter this type of mucky-muck should take the initiative to facilitate discussions where the facts and various perspectives can be conveyed. It is best to do this while maintaining a neutral and professional demeanor and by focusing on solving the problem (not on how this situation arose).

Variation 4: Undiscussables

Several members of the senior management team drove back to the office after an all-day off-site strategic planning meeting. As was typical, the meeting had been fine but lacked any real value. The lieutenant governor had asked for input, but he had only received a watered-down version of the managers' ideas, concerns, and complaints. Three fears had kept the managers from being honest about what they thought were the major problems in the agency. First, they did not want to upset the lieutenant governor and make the rest of the day (and week) more difficult. Second, the managers did not feel comfortable saying they disagreed with some decisions that had been made by their bosses. Third, they feared that discussing their personal frustrations could damage their careers and standing with the executives.

"Undiscussable" topics may include feelings and opinions about the organization, the work, and individual employees and customers. These undiscussables are common knowledge, such as the incompetent boss who got his promotion through nepotism or the low salary scale that erodes morale and makes it impossible to retain the best employees, but they are never verbalized or publicly acknowledged. Undiscussables are those issues that people are thinking about but that are too delicate, embarrassing, uncomfortable, or scary to discuss openly in a group setting. The problem is that these issues are being discussed by staff at the water cooler, over lunch, and behind closed doors.

There are two ways for middle managers to ensure that undiscussables don't get in the way of how they manage and lead. The first and more direct approach is to acknowledge the undiscussable. As a middle manager, you have the responsibility to be open and objective. This includes having the courage and conviction to take on tough topics. It is unlikely that you will lose your job or have your stature lowered for being open and honest (as long as it is constructive). Most undiscussables should be handled using the direct approach.

The second and less direct approach is to facilitate having certain individuals bring up the topic in the most palatable way. For example, a company president once asked a particular board member to attend a planning meeting because he was certain the board chair would be more responsive to ideas offered by that board member. Granted, this approach smacks a little of politics, but in some work environments it might be the most effective way for you to get results.

Variation 5: Disorganization

When Sally joined the agency, it took her two months to sort through her predecessor's piles of paper and disorganized files to discover what was going on. Meanwhile, she missed several deadlines she was unaware even existed. There was no work plan or project calendar to reference. Middle managers who take over a new function often face this form of mucky-muck. When misplaced data, buried files, or rarely seen desktops get in the way of completing a task, the work environment suffers from disorganization. Disorganization can affect an individual, a team, or an entire function or agency. Middle managers can get a handle on disorganization by creating a team event around getting organized. Have a Friday afternoon desk cleanout event, or a once-a-month organizing extravaganza. What you don't want to do is let getting organized wait—there may be something important and urgent on the bottom of one of those stacks of paper.

Variation 6: Learned Helplessness

Tim was struck by how listless, compliant, and dependent several of his employees were. They seemed like intelligent and dedicated people, but they did not demonstrate an ability to think independently or be enthusiastic about the work. Tim learned that the previous two managers had discouraged initiative and rewarded those who were compliant. Many in his group thus demonstrated learned helplessness, which occurs when a person or group accepts a certain reality based on previous experiences or information (when performance falls to meet low expectations). In the work environment, learned helplessness is common, and it is most often faced by middle managers who take over managing a team of people who have previously not performed well. Learned helplessness can be unlearned when the middle manager communicates and clarifies expectations and roles, and then follows up with training and reinforcement of the new expectations. By asking employees for their input (versus being directive), middle managers can help raise the expectations the employees have of themselves.

Variation 7: Hidden Agendas

Debbie called a meeting with the program managers to share her idea for a new community program. Though her concept was interesting, the managers could not help but wonder about her real motivation for the proposed change. Perhaps what she really wanted was for her group to lead the new program because she thought it would be more exciting and interesting than maintaining their current service programs.

Middle managers often work with people who have hidden agendas. These hidden agendas become a problem when they get in the way of others doing their jobs or relating in a genuine way. The reason a person acts a certain way or makes a particular decision is often a mystery. However, hidden agendas often revolve around power, being right, getting ahead, looking good to the boss, covering up a failure, or gaining support for a pet project. Hidden agendas can often be revealed by asking open-ended questions about the intent, benefits, and evolution of the idea or project. A middle manager's objective is not necessarily to eliminate hidden agendas but rather to understand them so that he or she can make a well-informed decision.

Variation 8: Long-Term Alliances

Corky had done her homework. Her detailed and well-researched proposal recommended changing a major employee benefit vendor. Making the change would save the agency money and would provide better service to its employees. It seemed to be a win-win situation. Little did Corky know that the current vendor, which charged premium rates and provided only average service, had a long-standing personal relationship with the finance director. Sure enough, what should have been a foolproof proposal failed miserably. Because middle managers interact with managers at all levels of the organization, it is inevitable that they will encounter this breed of mucky-muck. Old relationships or alliances can thwart productivity when they get in the way of sound business decisions or make the workplace dysfunctional. The best defense against being blindsided by long-term alliances is to ask questions early in the project planning process.

Variation 9: Burned Bridges

Lou was mortified. He had accidentally sent an email message disparaging a coworker to that very coworker! Though Lou apologized, he could not reverse the damage done to the relationship. As a middle manager, you may need to deal with burned bridges—whether your own or those of others in your department. Burned bridges get in the way of future communication and collaboration. The problem can get worse when other employees in the department get embroiled in the messy matter. To prevent burning a bridge with a peer or manager, never say or write anything that you would not feel comfortable repeating to that person directly. In particular, resist the urge to send inflammatory or emotional emails.

Variation 10: Clashes in Style

Dana and Sally were intelligent and dedicated managers who could not communicate effectively with each other. They conversed with each other in patronizing and disrespectful tones. However, when they worked with other people, everything was fine. The breakdown only occurred when they interacted with each other. Why did Dana and Sally have this problem? Their communication and behavioral styles clashed so severely that they annoyed each other and were unable to communicate effectively. They also lacked mutual respect, a situation that often accompanies a clash in styles.

High-impact managers need to be part psychologist and part mediator when faced with employees or coworkers whose styles clash and get in the way of their working relationship. Unfortunately, this makes work more difficult for everyone who has to compensate for those individuals. If you focus on the task at hand and not the way in which the other person presents his or herself, you will be more successful in dealing with clashes in style. Recognizing and being open about style differences will help disarm the power and magnitude of the clash.

Variation 11: Disempowerment

Overwhelmed and in danger of losing her job, Jane was not getting her work done on time. Jane's employees, on the other hand, had time and capacity to spare. In particular, Kathy had a strong background and work experience that could have helped Jane with several of the larger projects she was unable to complete on schedule. In fact, based on the scope of Kathy's job, at least one of the projects should have been her responsibility in the first place; but Jane chose to take it on herself because the work was interesting. Had Jane asked her to, Kathy could have done much of the work and planning; and the project would have been completed on time.

Disempowerment results in workload problems for the manager who is taking on more than he or she should. To recognize and reduce the effects of disempowerment, middle managers should periodically review roles and team member workloads with their manager and team. For each to-do item on your list, ask the question, "Should I be doing this, or does it belong on someone else's list?"

Aside from the loss of productivity, there are other disadvantages to disempowerment. Middle managers who disempower their employees lessen their intrinsic motivation and job satisfaction. It also causes role ambiguity, workflow disruptions, and miscommunication.

Variation 12: Contradictory Information

Mike was frustrated because he was not getting answers about why program usage had dropped dramatically from last year. Lou and Tim, the middle managers in charge of this program, were supposed to provide analysis and an action plan for getting back on track. The problem was that Tim and Lou did not see the significant drop that Mike did. In fact, some of their data suggested that use had actually increased from the previous year. The accounting department was working on providing a new and more accurate report, but it was running into contradictions and inconsistencies in the data. Two months had passed, and Mike was worried that the opportunity to fix the situation would evaporate. Meanwhile, Lou and Tim weren't even convinced that a problem existed.

Middle managers spend countless hours trying to find and validate the information they use to make decisions. Working with contradictory information is frustrating and wastes precious time. Worse yet, incorrect information can cause major errors in judgment and decisions. Middle managers who ask questions about how information is collected and take the initiative to analyze important measurements within their areas of responsibility are less likely to be affected by contradictory information. It is rarely a good strategy to assume that no news is good news concerning fundamental department processes.

Variation 13: Duplication of Efforts

Todd talked to Jake about creating an auditing process to ensure that products were meeting customer expectations. Lilly, as part of her overall project planning and improvement responsibilities, was also working on a new auditing process. When she found out that Todd had gone to Jake with his idea for an auditing process, she asked Todd why he was working on it. Todd said that he saw a need and took it upon himself to put together a plan. He did not know that Lilly had planned to create and implement a similar process. Together, they eventually worked it out so only one process was developed; but in the interim, everyone's valuable time was wasted. It was also uncomfortable for Lilly, who felt as though Todd had taken initiative in her area of responsibility.

Middle managers' responsibilities often overlap, but duplications of effort are wasteful and disruptive to the organization. Sometimes, as in the example of Lilly and Todd, duplication occurs because of misinformation. Other times, duplications occur because one manager does not have confidence in another—a hidden agenda for sure! Peers who regularly get together to share projects and priorities are less likely to get tripped up by duplications of effort. In addition, middle managers should know and respect one another's roles and areas of responsibility.

Variation 14: Sticks-in-the-Mud

Charlie had been with the agency a long time, and he remembered when it had been much smaller and easier to manage. Any time a new idea for automating information or processes came up, he would balk at the idea. He didn't believe that the agency needed to go to such lengths. He believed that the methods of yesterday would serve the current organization just as well. Not all sticks-in-the-mud are long-term employees reminiscing about "the good old days"; however, they do share a dislike of change and are leery of new approaches. Middle managers who face this type of mucky-muck spend more time and energy enrolling others in efforts at change.

Sticks-in-the-mud can get in the way of progress and make implementing new ideas more difficult. Middle managers can deal with change-resistant people by frequently communicating the purpose, plan, and staff roles relative to the change. You need to make sure that all employees understand the change and the reasons for it. Much resistance is born out of misinformation. Ultimately, change-resistant employees should not be allowed to sabotage or get in the way of changes that have been agreed upon.

Variation 15: Group Defections

Ron and his management team made all the right comments when they participated in agency-wide training meetings. They even seemed positive and optimistic about announced changes. However, when they returned to their workplace, it was as if none of these conversations had taken place. The members of Ron's management team decided that they would do the work their own way and ignored a lot of the communication that came from the executive office. Together, they essentially defected from the overall management team and became their own separate entity. As a result, their service area did not reflect the overall vision of the agency, and employees who transferred to their unit from other departments did not do well.

Group defections are more common in organizations than one would think, and they cause breaks in communication, work inefficiencies, and lower morale and employee satisfaction. Middle managers can eliminate group defections by ensuring that they spend time with each of their work teams and handle concerns and problems proactively. It is not enough to manage through emails and staff meetings. High-impact managers know what's going on in the groups they manage, because they spend quality time building formal and informal relationships and partnerships with each team and manager.

Variation 16: Sabotage

Deirdre knew it was not going to work. She had told the members of the management team before they implemented the new process that it would make her group less efficient and that they felt confused by the new procedures. Other groups had implemented the new automated process with few problems and had reduced processing times using the new system. Deirdre's manager, Bob, felt that she had caused the project to fail by disparaging the change to her team. She had practiced a form of subtle sabotage when she spoke negatively about the change to her employees. She had even encouraged them to help her amass evidence to keep things the way they were.

Most middle managers have experienced sabotage at one time or another. The most common forms of sabotage are negative and inappropriate comments about changes or decisions that have been made. Sabotage harms productivity, communication, and morale. Middle managers can reduce the likelihood of sabotage by being highly visible and accessible during times of change and by closely monitoring change implementation. Visibility will increase the manager's opportunity to observe and notice the subtle clues that a team member is not doing his or her part to support the change.

Summing Up

Do any of these forms of mucky-muck sound familiar? There is a practical reason for classifying these barriers as mucky-muck. Each represents weak, immature, or shortsighted behavior on the part of an individual, group, or organization. Mucky-muck does not make sense—it just is. This is not to say that it does not matter or cause damage. In some work environments, the mucky-muck is so thick that it drives smart people away or causes them to fail. Studying these characterizations of workplace folly will help you tackle it. In addition, when called "mucky-muck," a ridiculous name, to be sure, its power dwindles. Like calling a seven-foot muscle builder "Tiny," calling these barriers mucky-muck lessens their ability to intimidate. Mucky-muck is inevitable, but you can have a significant impact on how much mucky-muck there is and how your staff responds to it.

Eleven Techniques for Navigating Mucky-Muck

Teams rely on their managers to cut through the mucky-muck and help them get their jobs done. Middle managers are most likely to face mucky-muck because they interact with more functions, levels, groups, and individuals than do others in the agency. Once mucky-muck presents itself, you can reduce its power over your department and organization. High-impact managers have figured out how to best respond to mucky-muck so it does not get in the way of results. Let's look at 11 high-impact management techniques for navigating through the mucky-muck.

Technique 1: Do the Right Homework

Jim and his team needed to come up with a department plan for the coming year. They knew that senior management had several preconceived ideas about what the plan should look like. Rather than wasting their time creating a plan that only represented what they thought the priorities should be, they first sought to understand the senior managers' points of view, and then they developed their plan. Some might say this approach was faulty because it led to Jim and his team circumscribing their own ideas to those of senior management. Though this may be true, the team knew that the senior managers had already made up their minds about what they thought needed to happen. The team members knew that they could most help the organization by developing a plan that implemented senior management's ideas in the best possible way. In the end, they were able to influence several aspects of the plan much more than they would have had they not been sensitive to senior management's agendas.

As a middle manager, you will face situations like this on a regular basis. If there are strong opinions or relationships influencing a decision maker, it is best to do your homework and discover what they are before wasting too much time working in an opposite direction. Before starting a project, ask yourself, "Is there historical information that would be helpful to know? What are senior management's thoughts on this project? What approaches have been suggested in the past? Are there preferred vendors or partners that should be maintained?" There may be times when this added work and research is not necessary and unencumbered creative thinking is possible. However, it is always better to err on the side of being prepared and doing your homework.

Technique 2: Pick and Choose Your Battles

Ann knew that she was right about the benefits of changing to a different vendor and that she had presented a thorough case to her bosses. She felt the decision to turn down her proposal was not logical. She did not want to let go of her idea, but in the end she realized that it was not a battle worth fighting. The current vendor cost more and did not provide the high level of service that the proposed vendor would have; but overall, the service they received was satisfactory. Nothing terrible was going to happen if they kept the current vendor. There would be bigger and more important battles to fight another day, and Ann knew it was better to let this one go.

Middle managers often face the decision whether to hold firm and fight for what they think is right or accept another decision and move on. If you wage too many battles, you may end up commanding less respect in your organization. In addition, your message will seem watered-down and ineffective. Like the story of the boy who cried wolf, if you tout every proposal or idea as critically important, you will eventually find that the truly important projects will be ignored or seen as being unworthy of special consideration. High-impact managers know how to choose their battles and use their influence for maximum gain and consequence.

Technique 3: Focus Energy Where It Will Count

Tracy and her team knew there were a few departments that were not receptive to the coaching and development they could provide. She offered their services to all departments but focused on working with the few groups that showed interest in, and would most benefit from, their support. At any time, the other groups could change their mind and receive help as well. Tracy recognized that the saying "You can lead a horse to water, but you can't make it drink" also applied to individual managers and teams. By not forcing her support onto the managers who were obviously not interested in working with her, Tracy was able to spend her time in a way that was more fruitful and satisfying.

Middle managers work hard to have a positive influence on as broad an audience as possible. When individuals or groups show that they are not receptive, focus your efforts and attention in another direction. This, of course, is not always possible. If a middle manager finds that the people who report directly to him or her are not receptive to management, then he or she needs to address and fix the problem. The manager cannot choose to manage another group instead. If, however, there are several possible projects to propose and work on, it is wise to consider which will receive more collaboration and cooperation when deciding how to manage your and your team's time and resources.

Technique 4: Overcommunicate, Be Inclusive, and Follow Up

Lou assumed that other managers understood his role and the functions of which he had ownership. It is rarely safe to assume that this kind of interdepartmental understanding exists. A better approach for Lou would have been to communicate more frequently and with a wider audience about the projects and initiatives that he and his group were undertaking. All middle managers should err on the side of overcommunication to reduce the likelihood of miscommunication, duplication of work, and contradictory information.

Technique 5: Analyze and Fix It

When Mike joined the organization as the accounting manager, it was fraught with contradictory financial information and inaccurate reports. He rolled up his sleeves, dug into the numerical mess, and fixed many of the problems with the data. He also oversaw the creation of several reports that helped managers run their parts of the agency more effectively. When faced with contradictory information, duplication of efforts, or miscommunication, great middle managers do whatever it takes to understand and solve the problem. Good analysis goes a long way toward reducing or eliminating these and other types of mucky-muck.

Technique 6: Ask Probing Questions to Reveal Motives and Hidden Agendas

Mindy was an intuitive manager who knew the right questions to ask to discover a person's real intent and motivation. At one meeting, a manager was recommending that they restructure several roles. Mindy asked several questions to determine this manager's motive for recommending the change. Privately, she speculated whether his agenda was to increase the size of his organization or if he thought the current department manager was doing a poor job. Mindy's open-ended questions helped to clarify the details of the manager's recommendation. High-impact managers know when and how to ask the right questions that help explain the intent and motivation behind others' comments and suggestions.

Technique 7: Repair Relationships

John and Barry knew that their relationship was dysfunctional, but it was not until they were honest with each other that they were able to repair it and work together more effectively. Once they resolved issues between them, both of their departments experienced less mucky-muck.

It can be uncomfortable and difficult, but it is important for you to repair damaged relationships with current employees or coworkers. When not dealt with, these poor relationships will get in the way of communication, work flow, and results. Repairing a relationship does not mean that you have to socialize with each other; it means being able to work together productively and collaboratively. Workplace relationships should facilitate rather than hinder productive work.

Technique 8: Believe in the Capacity People Have for Change and Learning

If Tim had not looked past his employees' learned helplessness, he might have written them off as poor performers. Instead, he created a work environment that nurtured creativity and initiative. It took a while, but most of the previously lethargic employees became more engaged and passionate about their work. They accepted the changes that Tim was implementing and offered ideas for additional improvements. Great middle managers know that most performance problems are actually management or system problems and that, given the right guidance and leadership, nearly all employees will have the desire and capacity to do a great job. Mucky-muck can get in the way of people doing their best work, but the damage does not have to be permanent.

Technique 9: Get Organized

When Sally started her new job, she took over for an extremely unorganized manager. The first couple of months were difficult for Sally, and she felt set up to fail. Mucky-muck that comes from disorganization is common but is also the easiest kind to fix. Once Sally created a filing system and a routine that worked for her, she gained control of her department and became productive and successful. High-impact managers know that they need to stay organized to ensure that they and their teams are efficient and feel confident about their work. Whether done daily, weekly, or as needed, creating and practicing methods for organizing work is an important skill for middle managers. (Chapters 7 and 9 offer several techniques for staying organized.)

Technique 10: Lighten Up and Roll with It

Tim was an intense middle manager who let mucky-muck frustrate him. He asked why it was that things had to be a certain way or why it wasn't easier to get work done. This emotional reaction got in the way of his moving past the mucky-muck and getting his job done. It would have been better for him to shrug his shoulders, chuckle a bit, and rethink how to get the work done. Like Tim, some middle managers take mucky-muck too seriously. They get upset about the inefficiencies and frustration mucky-muck causes, which keeps them from being able to navigate through the mucky-muck. When dealing with mucky-muck, the first action you can take is to see it for the ridiculous barrier that it is. The middle managers who prevail despite it all are able to quickly move beyond the barriers. They know there are many ways to make a difference, and that they can do great work even when faced with mucky-muck. Sometimes, the best approach is just to laugh at it and move on.

Technique 11: See and Enjoy Accomplishments

Jim was grumbling to Lou about how hard it was to work in their organization because of all the mucky-muck he faced daily. Lou agreed but chose to see it another way. Although Jim was right about the mucky-muck, Lou saw the situation as inspiring and hopeful. They had a great middle management team that accomplished much under difficult working conditions. They had been successful in creating major change and improvements within a work environment that was rife with politics, disorganization, and other permeations of mucky-muck. What an accomplishment!

Moreover, they were learning skills that would benefit their careers and enable them to prevail in almost any work environment. Yes, it was frustrating, and, yes, getting things done should not have been so hard, but the success of the team was worthy of celebration. Middle managers who produce results and get through the mucky-muck should recognize and take pride in the work they do and the results they achieve against the odds.

Summing Up

High-impact managers practice these 11 techniques to reduce and eliminate mucky-muck from their work environment. They try to bring perspective to each challenge and strengthen weak communication channels that are often at the core of mucky-muck. These techniques are also excellent methods for managing other complex or emotionally charged situations. Once you practice seeing and managing mucky-muck, you will become skilled at recognizing emerging problems and preventing them from undermining morale and derailing projects.

Be Part of the Solution, Not the Problem

As a high-impact manager, you need to be careful that you do not become a mucky-muck generator. Now that it is clear what mucky-muck is and how it damages productivity and results, you have the responsibility to own the mucky-muck that you create and to eliminate it. There are significant benefits in doing so. First, your work will be more meaningful and successful when not deluged with self-inflicted mucky-muck. Second, middle managers who ensure that they do not become part of the problem will enjoy others' respect and trust. To make your workplace productive, use these guidelines:

- Plan and communicate work plans in clear and complete terms.
- Communicate openly and candidly with managers, peers, and employees.
- Understand the motivations and intentions behind your ideas and suggestions. Share them honestly.
- Share projects and initiatives with peers at the formative stage of planning and implementation.

- Be a good workplace citizen. Represent the organization and management team well.
- Support employees so they can fully take on and own the work appropriate to their job.

On the other hand, do not do the following:

- Gossip or bad-mouth others.
- Obstruct or otherwise subtly sabotage changes.
- Allow differences in style or personality to get in the way of working productively with a peer or employee.
- Interfere with or take over a project or task that one of your employees owns.
- Let work pile up or become disorganized.
- Play favorites or make decisions based on friendship.

By following these guidelines, you can have an immediate and positive impact on your work environment. Mucky-muck can be full of uncomfortable emotions, and dealing with them is draining. Reducing mucky-muck frees up mental and physical energy that can be used to do great work. Start calling the barriers you face mucky-muck in the presence of others and notice how referring to them in this silly way can help reduce their power and importance.

Chapter 7

Organizational Alignment: Ensuring That the Department Delivers Results

A well-aligned department hums with efficiency. Processes for getting the work done are clearly understood and effective. Staff members' roles support the goals of both their work team and the organization. Individuals are clear about what they should contribute. They are appropriately empowered and expected to produce results. Communication to and from departments facilitates each team's ability to remain on course and prioritize. The organizational structure and individual roles enable team members to identify and solve problems quickly. Work is more satisfying because it makes sense.

In contrast, poorly aligned organizational structures and processes cause numerous problems with quality, throughput, and results. When a structure or process is out of alignment with the larger goal it was designed to support, it no longer serves the goals of the team and organization. Poor alignment can occur for various reasons. Perhaps changes have occurred in one area of the organization, but not in others. Sometimes the problem is a lack of effective processes for getting the work done. Or it could be that roles have changed but processes have not, or visa versa.

A common reason for poor alignment is conflict among technology, processes, and roles. For team members, a poorly aligned organization feels disorganized, and getting work done seems more difficult than it should. Ambiguous, confusing, and overlapping roles are also signs of poor alignment. The design and planning of workflow is significant and should be a major focus for middle managers. Many middle managers, however, assume that unproductive people are to blame for poor results. Though there may be personnel problems for the manager to resolve, it is more likely that the department's processes and structures are responsible for the poor results.

Elements of Organizational Structure

The organizational structure defines job roles, departmental interdependencies, and communication channels. Structure determines who makes the decisions, and the depth and breadth of each person's role. Structure assigns responsibilities and accountabilities. The high-impact management definition of a middle manager is someone who oversees and is responsible for at least one structure and/or function that exists within the larger organization's structure. For example, a middle manager who leads the sales and marketing departments may oversee a sales organization structure, a marketing structure, and one or more cross-functional project teams, each with their own structure. The human resources director may oversee one large structure that encompasses the entire department with several smaller structures supporting the functions of recruiting, benefits, and training.

Processes are ways of working within a structure. They may be as elaborate and complicated as a computer-controlled manufacturing line or as simple as a way to deliver mail throughout an office building. There are also de facto processes, or processes that have evolved and become standard practice without intentional design or planning. Most middle managers oversee several processes. Inefficient or irrelevant processes hurt results and cause productivity to suffer. This chapter will help middle managers ensure that they have the right structure and processes in place to produce results.

As a high-impact manager, you should continuously evaluate and realign structures and processes. Doing so will give you and your team the best chance for success. When results are inadequate, ask yourself, your team members, and your peers if the way the work is being done is enabling results or getting in the way of them. Are the processes and procedures that have been established setting you up for success or failure?

Best Practices for Organizational Alignment

High-impact management organizational alignment is a set of practices that enables middle managers to keep their structures and processes relevant and productive. These practices begin by looking at your department, and the work it produces, from a 50,000-foot-high view, or broad perspective, to answer one fundamental question: Is this department set up for success? High-impact managers regularly look at their functions in this way because they know that keeping roles and processes aligned is critical to ensuring optimal throughput and results. And although you might not have a lot of latitude to increase or reduce roles or projects, you certainly can take steps to improve the efficiency and alignment of your group based on current resourcing levels. Once the big picture is clear, you can begin to focus on aspects of the structures and processes that need attention to deliver results. Organizational alignment should follow these best practices:

- Clarify the vision, purpose, and goals of the department.
- Use clean slate creativity to design an ideal organization model.
- Compare the needs of the department, the ideal organizational model, and current roles and processes.
- Generate alternatives that improve the organization.
- Realign structure, processes, roles, and procedures for maximum efficiency.
- Measure and monitor processes and workflow.

High-impact management organizational alignment will help you ensure that your work structures and processes mesh in a way that enables team members to be their most productive and deliver results. Let's look at each of the six best practices.

Practice 1: Clarify the Vision, Purpose, and Goals of the Department

The middle manager, his or her manager, and team should all agree on the vision of the department's success and the expectations the organization has for the department (see chapter 5). These expectations should represent and reflect the needs and wants of both internal and external customers. The sidebar gives an example of what the vision, purpose, and goals might look like for an organization's accounting department.

The accounting department is an internal service group and has an opportunity and responsibility to provide responsive and helpful service to both internal and external customers. This includes providing accurate and timely information, proactive analysis, resolution of problems, and responses to questions. There is also an expectation that, as the accounting experts, the department's staff will ensure that the organization is following proper procedures to ensure fiscal accuracy and compliance with important regulations and audit principles. As the agency expands its presence on the Internet, it is expecting the accounting function to support and reconcile transactions produced via the web. Over the next year, the accounting team's major goals are to

- Improve the efficiency of invoice processing to reduce errors by 50 percent and improve processing speed by 15 percent, while at the same time maintaining or reducing current processing costs.
- Improve purchasing and payment processes related to field operations so that communications and information exchange are more efficient and the cost of the processing is reduced by 10 percent or more.
- Design and launch accurate and helpful reports that enable department managers to manage their areas more proactively and effectively. This effort should lead to an overall reduction in budget variances by the third month of implementation.
- Create and implement by June a strategy that supports the agency's plans for selling licenses on its website. Develop online cash register services and reconciliation methods to ensure the proper collection and management of revenues.

A department's statement of its vision, purpose, and goals is an important tool for middle managers. It should become part of the department's playbook (see chapter 5) and be posted for employees, peers, and managers to see. When you take the time, as a middle manager, to crystallize and clarify your department's vision, purpose, and goals, you build a foundation for creating organizational alignment.

Practice 2: Use Clean Slate Creativity to Design an Ideal Organization Model

To realign structures and processes, it is important to start the design process with a clean slate before considering current resources, processes, and roles. Using clean slate creativity means designing, from the ground up, the ideal way a team and its processes should function to produce the vision and goals (see the sidebar for more details). For this exercise, do not think about current personnel, roles, resources, or processes. Instead, you should define how the work would be designed if nothing were already in place—hence the clean slate metaphor. These questions will help get your creative juices flowing:

- What is the long-term direction of the agency, and how should the manager and team design today's work with this in mind?
- What is the most important work this team could do?
- What needs to be accomplished to meet or exceed the team's goals? Look at each goal individually, then look at the goals as a whole.
- To do this work, what roles are required? How should the department divide work among individuals and teams?
- How should managers and team members make decisions?
- What should the key processes be, and how should they work? What processes would make the work easier and more efficient?
- What role should technology play?
- How would the team and processes link to the rest of the agency?
- What are the advantages and disadvantages of this organizational design?

- What human, process, and technological resources are needed to make this organizational structure work?
- If there were no limitations on resources, how would you and your team design the department's structure?

If it is feasible, you may find it helpful to have the entire team contribute to creating this design. The product of this creative work is an ideal view of what the work group and processes would look like if designed from scratch to produce the department's vision, purpose, and goals. In addition to the clarifying roles, it is important to identify the processes that would make the team's work easier and more efficient. Depending on the scope and breadth of the work you are assessing, this exercise could take several hours or even days.

Clean Slate Creativity versus Problem Solving

There are two distinct ways you, as a middle manager, can approach a situation that needs improvement. You can choose clean slate creativity or employ a problem-solving approach. In using the clean slate approach, define how you would manage the work if there were no processes currently in place and no limitations on resources. To be successful using this method, do not to let your ideas become bogged down or hampered by current processes, people, or corporate culture. You can recognize current resources and limitations later in the redesign process.

When using a problem-solving approach, begin with today's roles, processes, and circumstances, and then define ways to improve results or performance from this current reality. Ideas conceived using this approach will more likely be similar and complementary to the work and processes your department is already using. Thus, the problem-solving approach works best when your department only needs to make minor changes or adjustments, not redesign an organization or process. Ideas that come from clean slate creativity will be more innovative, more creative, and more likely to lead to significant improvements in productivity.

Middle managers should complete this clean slate creativity exercise for their entire department at least once every two years, and then follow up with smaller redesign efforts for specific areas as needed. For example, if your agency launches a new community service, a portion of the department's work and processes may need realignment. If there is one available, having a facilitator guide you and your team through these conversations is often helpful and allows a middle manager to participate fully.

Practice 3: Compare Department Needs, the Ideal Plan, and Current Roles and Processes

Once the ideal organizational design is complete, middle managers will be ready to bring the current reality into the realignment process and conversation. It is important to include a discussion of de facto processes—meaning those processes that you and your and team have not purposefully designed or implemented but that have developed over time. There are generally many more processes in place than middle managers recognize. For example, communication and problem resolution are areas where de facto processes are common.

During this part of the realignment, you will need to blend the ideal scenario with current roles, personnel, and processes. There is always going to need to be some give and take and some compromises. It is important to stand firm and resolute for the changes that are most important and be flexible and nimble in areas where multiple approaches might work. You and your team should answer these questions:

- How far apart are the ideal organizational model and the current organization? What are the differences and similarities?
- Is the ideal organization possible and practical?
- If the ideal organization is worth attaining, what might a transitional organization look like? How can the department begin its journey to ideal alignment?
- What aspects of the current organization and processes should not be changed? (Challenge the thinking behind the answers to these questions.) Why should these processes or roles stay the same?

- What further information or research do you and your team need to understand these ideas and choices? (Do this analysis and research before making decisions.)
- What objections or concerns will senior managers or peers have about these ideas? Are they valid? How can you and your team overcome these objections?

Again, using a facilitator to guide you and your team through this process is helpful and advised. A facilitator can see where the team is getting bogged down and where its thinking might need to be challenged. If a facilitator is not available, you will need to do a thorough job of planning the agenda and discussion questions before the meeting. After this conversation, you will know the ideas that have been placed on the table and the pros and cons of each. You will also have a good idea of how much needs to change to create alignment. This is a useful and illuminating process.

A word about team member participation: The general rule is that you should include input from team members and peers as much as possible. Depending on the nature of the realignment, it may not be appropriate to include team members in discussions about redesigning roles and processes. If jobs might be eliminated, then team members should not participate in the final design of roles. If team members ask whether jobs might be cut (they are probably wondering, even if they do not ask), it is best to be open and honest. You can say that the purpose of the organizational realignment and redesign is to figure out how the department can be more efficient and effective. This may mean that some processes and jobs will change or be affected, but the final details will not be clear until the realignment plan is complete and approved. If people are likely to be affected, middle managers should get through the redesign process as quickly as possible. If the organizational realignment is going to be significant and include major role changes, it might be best to complete the entire redesign process confidentially and without team member participation. Middle managers who do not include team members in the redesign process should take extra care and caution to ensure that they are getting thorough and accurate information with which to make decisions.

Practice 4: Generate Alternatives for Organizational Improvement

As a middle manager you should create two or three realignment approaches based on the information collected and the discussion that has occurred. If there is one alternative that seems significantly better than the other possible plans, then present only one plan. Because there is often more than one workable scenario, it is generally best to prepare and present more than one option. As the planning progresses, you may eliminate choices based on several criteria including cost, ease of use, technology, and mucky-muck. The exception to this rule is when the middle manager and team feel confident and positive about an organizational design they have created. If you have done your homework and included the appropriate people in discussions, then present this recommendation and sell it to the key stakeholders and decision makers. Energy and passion account for much of the success of any plan. Whether presenting one or more alternatives, each plan should include

- a review of the vision, purpose, and goals the realignment seeks to support
- the major reasons the realignment is necessary
- a review of the proposed realigned organization and processes, and the results that the proposed organization will produce
- transition plans for personnel roles and processes that would change
- a description of roles and interdependencies between team members
- a description of major processes
- an explanation of how the work will flow from and to other groups
- a breakdown of costs, including short-term and long-term cost effects.

Depending on the scope of the plan, preparing it could take anywhere from a few hours to a couple of weeks. For a narrow focus area or single process, the entire realignment can take less than a day. Don't rush the process if more analysis and creativity will make the plan significantly richer or better. As the plan is coming together, middle managers should play the devil's advocate and encourage team members to challenge it to ensure that it answers potential objections and meets the needs of supporters and potential naysayers. Present the options to several trusted peers and ask for their input. Adjust the plan as appropriate.

Present the plan and gain approval! Provide backup information and details as needed. Have this information ready and available when others ask questions. Take the time to prepare for the presentation of the plan, because this will speed up its approval. Be open to adjusting the plan to get full support.

Practice 5: Realign Structure, Processes, Roles, and Procedures

The implementation of new structures and processes is critical to the success of the realignment. To ensure that team members and peers support the new way of doing the work, middle managers should

- Work with management and human resources on the timing of the plan's implementation, especially if any individual jobs or positions are affected.
- Communicate the vision, the realignment plan, the transition plan, and the role of each team member. Discuss the plan with peers and gain their support. If an individual's job is changing significantly, talk with him or her one-to-one before making any team announcements.
- Create a project plan for the transition of roles and processes. Ensure that all team members and affected peers have a current copy of the plan. Hold daily or weekly progress chats as needed.
- Be sincerely open and ready to listen to any concerns, suggestions, or questions. Be flexible enough to accept that the plan may need to be altered. Take time every day to check in with team members and peers. Do not micromanage the process, but show support and invite feedback.

Practice 6: Measure and Monitor Processes and the Work Flow

As the realignment rolls out and takes hold, it is important to monitor and measure performance and productivity. After all, increased efficiency and effectiveness are why changes were made in the first place! Figures should be communicated clearly and discussed often. As well as being part of the departmental playbook, key figures and milestones should be posted in a visible place in the department. If team members are located in the field, you can send figures and results to each team member and discuss them during regular email and telephone conversations.

Ensuring that your department is set up for success is important work for middle managers. Team members are more productive and satisfied when roles and processes facilitate results. In an aligned organization, mucky-muck goes down and the work environment is more intrinsically motivating.

An aligned organization runs like a well-oiled machine. High-impact managers know that to ensure their teams are set up for success, processes and roles need to be evaluated regularly as changes occur. When processes are inefficient, they produce waste and cause team members to work harder to get results. When roles are unclear or do not encompass new expectations, team members cannot do their best work. The high-impact management organizational alignment will help middle managers get results efficiently.

High-Impact Leaders Are Unstoppable! Wiping Out Limitations to Results

Marty was talented, and creative—a great catch for the agency. He was hired to take over the leadership of an internal service department that was not meeting its deadlines and producing low-quality work. He had the right vision and understood the importance of delivering high-quality work that was on time and on budget. Thus, his managers were puzzled when the timeliness of the department's work went from bad to worse under his management.

To ensure that the planning, timeliness, and quality of the work was acceptable, Marty oversaw and reviewed all the work his group produced. Everything flowed through him and relied on his stamp of approval. Because quality was an issue and he wanted to develop his team's ability to recognize and solve problems, he reworked many of the projects himself. The quality of the work improved, but the completion rate was getting worse because he micromanaged every project. He also needed to spend time evaluating vendors and creating a long-term strategic plan for the department. There was not enough Marty to go around, and his involvement in projects had become a constraint.

Paul, another manager in Marty's agency, felt stuck. He needed to create and implement a plan to upgrade his team's skills and professionalism, but he put off the work again and again. He turned down help when it was offered. Time slipped away and he did not have his plan ready or implemented in time to secure the resources he needed. He didn't know how to plan well. He had a tendency to be reactive instead of proactive, and he was often uncoachable when the topic of planning or time management came up. He often let the needs of the day divert his attention, and he never got around to completing the plan.

Corky knew she needed to get candidates through the selection and hiring process more quickly and efficiently, but she was at a loss about where to start. The recruiting process had many parts, each a potential place for breakdowns and delays. The application flow was good, but sometimes the applications sat for a while before anyone had time to review them. At times, interviews took longer than expected because of schedule conflicts. Reference checks, background checks, and drug screenings took more time than Corky preferred, but these processes relied on outside vendors who would not commit to faster results. The best candidates also needed to give their current employer two weeks' notice before leaving. Corky wondered what changes she could make that would optimize the hiring process while taking into account the resources available to her.

Maximizing Throughput

Marty, Paul, and Corky struggled with challenges that limited their results. Maximizing throughput to deliver products and services is an important responsibility of all middle managers. Throughput is the rate at which a person, department, system, or function produces results. Throughput may be expressed in terms of speed, quantity, time, or a combination of these factors. Most work can be described in terms of throughput. The time it takes to make decisions is throughput. The number of completed calls may be throughput. The accuracy of completed payroll check runs is throughput. Manager capacity can even be thought of in terms of throughput.

Middle managers are in the best position to recognize and resolve problems that limit throughput because they see and interact with many levels and layers of work, systems, and processes. In addition, it makes sense for middle managers to be concerned with and interested in throughput, because throughput leads to results. Middle managers are often the most directly accountable for producing results. Focusing on and improving throughput may come naturally to some middle managers; those who come from a traditional manufacturing or product distribution background are most likely to have had experience in this area. Many middle managers, however, have had neither training nor experience in solving throughput problems.

A disciplined and focused day-to-day management practice is essential to understanding and improving throughput. Once major problems are resolved, middle managers should still be prepared to monitor and troubleshoot throughput on a regular basis. Factors that limit throughput may change daily or be a continuing problem. In either case, middle managers who are prepared to quickly identify and deal with these problems get better results. Middle managers must seek out and remove barriers to throughput, using analysis, conversation, observation, and interactive "management by walking around."

What Reduces Throughput?

Several common work practices and actions can limit throughput. Sometimes making one change can improve throughput; while at other times, combining several actions will work best. You should also be cautious about making changes. For example, making a change in one area may cause problems in other areas. There are several ways to look at throughput, and each offers a unique view of potential problems and limiting factors. No one approach is likely to be appropriate all the time. The most important skill for middle managers is to be able to recognize what is getting in the way of results. Learning this skill can sometimes be a challenge and may require that a middle manager use more than one "model," or way of looking at how the work gets done. Let's look at the eleven most common types of problems affecting throughput and a sampling of approaches used for solving them.

Problem 1: Bottlenecks

A bottleneck is a point of congestion that reduces the flow of work and hinders progress and productivity. One way to recognize a bottleneck is by the work that piles up before the bottleneck and the people or process steps that are waiting for work coming from the bottleneck. There may be more than one bottleneck in a workflow or process. Figure 8-1 shows a simple process. Steps B and C are bottlenecks because they cannot process as much work as can steps A and D. If step A consistently pushes at a rate of 25 per day and step B at a rate of 20, work will pile up before steps B and C; and step D will sometimes be idle, or pulling on step C for more work.

Figure 8-1. A Simple Process with Two Bottlenecks

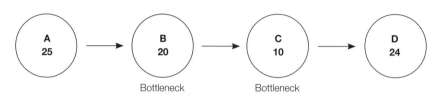

Figure 8-2 shows another common situation that produces bottlenecks. In this example, three separate processes all use the same resource, step C/L/S. A resource can be a person, a process step, a piece of machinery, or a computer function. This resource can handle the workload of any one process, but not all three. Step C/L/S is a major bottleneck. Steps J, K, B, and Q are also bottlenecks.

The story about Marty at the beginning of this chapter was an example of a bottleneck created when a resource serves multiple processes. Marty supported all processes in his department; but as a single resource, he could not keep up with the demands from upstream and downstream customers and suppliers.

Problem 2: Constraints

A constraint is the bottleneck that has the most impact on overall throughput and results. There is only one constraint in a process or system (unless there are two bottlenecks that have the same throughput rate). In fact, one constraint may affect several processes. A constraint can be a person, system, process step, piece of machinery, or computer function. In the previous example, Marty is both a bottleneck and a constraint.

Figure 8-2. Three Processes with a Common Bottleneck

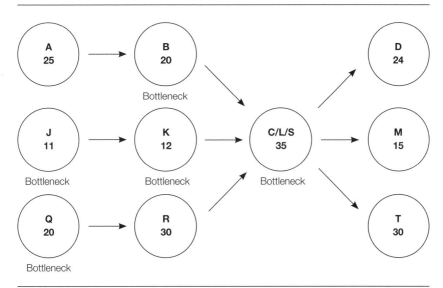

Figure 8-3 shows a simple process with both the bottlenecks and the constraint identified. Step C is the constraint because it has the most impact on output. This process has a throughput of 10, because that is the capacity of the constraint. Remember the saying "A chain is only as strong as its weakest link"? The same logic holds true for throughput. The process step with the lowest capacity sets the pace of throughput. It is not always easy to find the constraint.

In figure 8-3, the answer is simple. Looking at figure 8-2 again, it is not clear which step is the constraint. To decide this, the manager will

Figure 8-3. A Bottleneck and Constraint

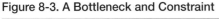

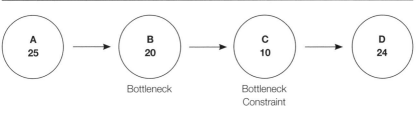

need to calculate the time the C/L/S resource spends on each process vying for its time. If C = 10, L = 10 and S = 15, then this resource is the constraint for all three processes. If C = 23, L = 12 and S = 0, the C/L/S resource would be the constraint for the Q/R/S/T process (in fact, this process has stalled) but not for the other two processes. In this case, step B and step J are the constraints for the other two processes. If Marty is the C/L/S resource, it would help to identify how he spends his time and how his choices are affecting each project or process that relies on him. It is common for middle managers to spread their time evenly and become a bottleneck or constraint in many work processes or to focus on one or two projects and become the constraint on others. Neither of these approaches maximizes throughput.

Problem 3: Slow Process Connections

Sometimes the connections between resources affect throughput more than the steps of the process itself. This is particularly a problem with work processes that rely on two or more handoffs between people in the same or different departments. Figure 8-4 shows a three-step process with two handoffs.

The process steps to make a purchase add up to a total time of three to four days. However, the total order processing time is much longer, as much as 8 to 11 days, or up to almost three times longer! Process connections can often account for as much as or more than the total throughput time spent in the process steps. It is common for work to sit and wait for

Figure 8-4. A Three-Step Process with Two Handoffs

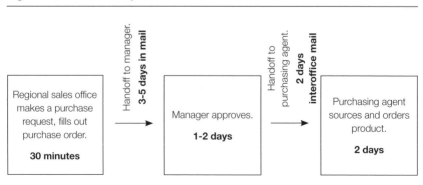

the next person or process step to move it forward. Much of the time spent between process steps is wasted and is a common cause of reduced throughput. Processes with many steps are particularly vulnerable to the effects of slow process connections. It is important to define the time used by process connections and process steps, because the methods for improving throughput are different depending on where the inefficiencies lie.

Problem 4: Lengthy or Complicated Critical Paths

A critical path shows the minimum amount of time a process or project will take to be completed by identifying interdependent steps. Dependencies among steps slow processes. For example, if new computers cannot be purchased until the capital budget is approved, then the work on installing new computers is dependent on the budget approval; and this has to be taken into account when determining the time it will take to complete the project. Some work can occur concurrently, while other work depends on the completion of a previous step. A critical path shows middle managers which interdependencies are affecting the overall throughput rate.

Figure 8-5 shows a simple critical path. In this example, the minimum critical path is six weeks and four days long. In other words, if everything goes well, and assuming the process connections are efficient, the work will take no less than six weeks and four days. Steps A, B, D, and F are on the critical path. They set the pace of results because of their dependency on one another. Step B cannot begin until step A is complete. Step F cannot begin until step D is complete, but it can begin concurrently with step E. Step C can begin after step A, but then it does not affect other steps.

Remember Corky from earlier in the chapter? She needed to improve the speed and efficiency of the hiring process. It is likely that the process suffered from a long critical path and that she would have to change this to make any real improvements to hiring throughput. Figure 8-6 illustrates what her hiring process looked like.

The critical path for the hiring process is a minimum of 24 days long! This assumes there is a steady stream of applications and that the

Figure 8-5. A Simple Critical Path

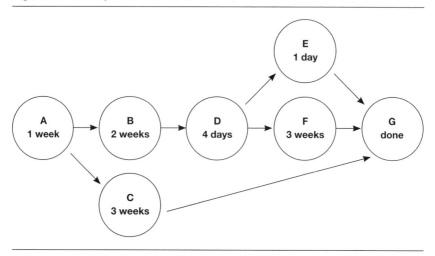

recruiter does not need to advertise the position. If there are not enough applicants, the hiring process is 30 to 35 days long. Given that most employees provide a two weeks' notice before leaving the organization, it is difficult for Corky's team to meet the organization's needs. The critical path for her hiring process is too long and does not serve her goal of having new employees in place when needed.

Problem 5: Skills Deficiencies

One of the more common reasons for slower throughput of general work assignments and projects is a middle manager's inability to plan, monitor, and assign work. When middle managers have not learned the skills needed to organize and prioritize work, they put off the wrong tasks and waste time fighting preventable fires.

Paul did not plan well and this got in the way of his success. He worked hard and cared about the quality and success of his team. What he could not see was that his inability to make better time management choices hurt his department and his career. He had a long to-do list, but he failed to realize that all his tasks were not equal. He did not have the experience or know-how to recognize important critical paths. To start the new project off well, he needed to be planning and making several important decisions six months in advance.

Figure 8-6. Corky's Hiring Process

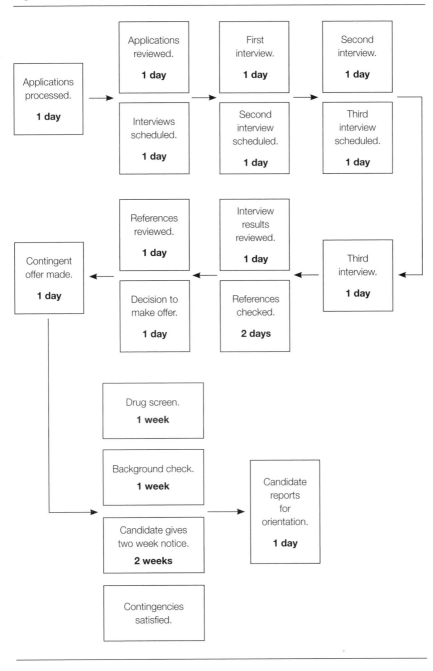

Instead, Paul spent his time on what was most pressing in his mind, which was work on a project due in a month. That work was important, too, but he could have delegated it or delayed working on it for a week or two. He needed to create the departmental plan; however, by the time he got around to thinking about it, several important deadlines had passed. Inexperienced middle managers, like Paul, often do not feel the sense of urgency when it comes to planning and do not understand that the lead time needed for planning is just as important a deadline as those for other pressing tasks. Middle managers need to be excellent planners and communicators to ensure that the work keeps flowing.

Other skills shortages also get in the way of throughput. Middle managers who have not developed their abilities to partner, manage performance, set goals, or coach others will also suffer from lower throughput. Other chapters of this book address these skills.

Problem 6: Breakdowns

Breakdowns are system or process failures. People can also be the cause of breakdowns. Personal illnesses, vacations, and other situations that cause a person to stop working on a task could be considered breakdowns. When Tim first looked at the throughput in his department, he found that an excessive use of sick days by several of his staff members caused lower productivity and work quality.

Problem 7: Errors

Errors are mistakes that cause work to have to be reworked or lead to other additional work. The library accounting department spent an average of six person-hours per week fixing accounts payable check run errors, or 5 percent of the team's total human resources! With a group of just three employees, this represents a significant waste of resources, which had a negative impact on their throughput.

Problem 8: Waste

Waste, as it relates to throughput, is work that is substandard or not usable—or work that, though satisfactory, is not used. When an employee copies and then distributes reports that few read, this is waste. The reports are usable, but few people are using them. It is also considered waste when marketing materials are scrapped due to inaccurate information. Waste uses resources that could otherwise be used for work that makes a difference. Waste reduces throughput potential. Reducing waste can be an easy and effective way to boost throughput without adding cost or resources.

Problem 9: Changes

Changes affect throughput in a variety of ways. When changes occur, error rates and waste may also increase. In addition, many changes result in temporary skills deficiencies and work pace slowdowns. Middle managers should take into account the potential impact that changes will have on throughput. Though some temporary productivity dips may be acceptable, a good middle manager should have some strategies in place for minimizing disruption.

Problem 10: Employee Turnover

Employee turnover results in skills deficiencies, higher error rates, slower work paces, breakdowns, and waste. Throughput is often disrupted when employees leave.

Problem 11: Inadequate Worker Training

When changes and improvements are made, workers need to be retrained. Some skills are specialized enough so that refresher training will improve throughput. When workers do not have the right training, they cannot do their best work.

Summing Up

Is it any wonder that your job is so tough? Many things affect throughput. One of your most challenging and important responsibilities as a middle manager is to do whatever is necessary to diagnose and solve these problems to improve results. However, deciding what action will make the most difference is not always easy or straightforward.

Becoming Unstoppable: Techniques for Improving Throughput

High-impact managers know how to zero in on problems affecting throughput. They focus on the areas posing the most significant challenges and systematically remove them or lessen their effect. The toughest part may be defining the problem. These techniques facilitate maximizing throughput and results when practiced regularly:

- Establishing a results-oriented environment.
- Diagnosing throughput problems.
- Solving throughput problems.
- Asking the right questions.

Establishing a Results-Oriented Environment

Middle managers who create work environments in which their employees quickly identify, openly discuss, and creatively solve problems will outproduce managers who do not. Managers cannot realistically expect to discover and tackle each problem themselves. When teams work together to ensure that nothing gets in the way of throughput, work is more productive and satisfying. Managers will know when this environment exists because improvements and problem solving happen naturally.

To create a results-oriented environment, middle managers should react positively and supportively to employees who bring problems to their attention. Do your employees feel comfortable discussing problems or errors? Do they feel sure that you care and want to know about the good, the bad, and the ugly? Do you provide negative reinforcement for raising questions or challenging ideas? Do your employees feel appreciated for their efforts to solve problems?

Case Study

Harry's employees did not share their ideas with him very often. His first and most natural response was to be defensive. Even when his staff was not laying blame in his direction, it seemed as though he took most any concern, criticism, or alternative idea as a personal censure. He also had a tendency to want to cover up problems in his area. Once, he had several managers who were bottlenecks to an important change the group was making. Instead of being open about this problem, he led senior management to believe that these managers backed the change effort and that there would be no problems with the implementation. When the senior managers later found out about the resistance, he said that he didn't know it existed—even though his staff had told him about it weeks earlier. He gave his managers no reason to be proactive in identifying and communicating problems or barriers. As a result, they were reactive, and their throughput suffered.

Middle managers who want to create a results-oriented work environment should be sure that they are accessible and responsive. Having regular and informal conversations with team members provides an opportunity for sharing news about the work. Managers who ask open-ended questions rooted in curiosity and support (versus those rooted in control) will discover people's concerns and ideas. Practicing management by walking around daily helps middle managers stay in tune with daily happenings. These social activities serve a practical purpose. Managers who know what is going on in their department can better react to areas that need their time and support. Managers who routinely close their office doors or are inaccessible are not using communication—one of the most valuable management tools to improve throughput.

Diagnosing Throughput Problems

There are many possible reactions to barriers or problems affecting throughput. Deciding which actions will provide the greatest benefit requires analysis and diagnosis. The 80/20 rule applies here. One or a few remedies (20 percent) will have a more significant impact (80 percent) on results than most other possible actions. Your goal is to determine which responses will have the maximum benefit. To do this, it is important to classify the type of limitations getting in the way of throughput. The following questions can help you decide how to focus their improvement efforts. Ask them with a process, system, or project in mind that is not experiencing satisfactory throughput:

- Is this process, system, or project plagued by bottlenecks?
- Is there more than one identifiable bottleneck?
- Is there a step, person, or part of the process that is holding up progress and forward movement of the work?
- Can you identify the constraint or the pacesetter?
- Is there a large difference between how long the work takes at each step and the total time of completion?
- Do handoffs between process or project steps take longer than wanted?
- Is the critical path too long?
- Are there opportunities to look at reducing dependencies between steps or tasks?
- Is the manager struggling to stay on top of the demands on his or her time?
- Does the manager lack practical experience or training in how to plan and communicate work?
- Is mucky-muck a major problem impacting productivity?
- Have there been any breakdowns or shutdowns that have affected this work?
- Is this process, project, or system plagued by errors?
- Does this process, system, or project waste time, energy, or resources?
- Has change had a negative impact on the work?
- Has the team working on this process, project, or system suffered from the turnover of personnel?
- Do any team members lack the skills to keep the work flowing?

For those questions to which the answers are unknown, take a moment to analyze and discover the answer. You may find that creating a worksheet with these questions and answers will help you to further clarify the issues. Taking the time to draw a diagram of the process or work flow can be enlightening as well. You can draw almost any work process or project using circles and arrows, as pictured in the figures earlier in this chapter. Be sure to define each process connection, because these handoffs are often a source of waste. Notice where the bottlenecks are and the single step or person that is the constraint. What is the pace of the constraint? If the pace is acceptable, then bottlenecks and constraints are not your primary problem. Next, try to create the critical path. When first defining a critical path, it is often surprising how many steps a process contains and how long the critical path is.

Each "yes" response in the worksheet suggests a possible focus for improvement. Once completed, the worksheet will help you evaluate various possible opportunities to improve throughput. Specific techniques that address areas of opportunity follow. After reviewing these suggestions, you will be able to determine which improvements will have the highest impact on results.

Eli Goldratt's Theory of Constraints

The author, scientist, and educator Eliyahu Goldratt has advanced the science and practice of understanding throughput, constraints, and bottlenecks. In his books—*The Goal, It's Not Luck,* and *Critical Chain*—he shares his theory of constraints in a way that is helpful to middle managers who want to improve their results. Middle managers who oversee numerous or major processes or projects will benefit from reading his books and learning about his theory of constraints. This book does not seek to teach or explain the theory of constraints; rather, it is a general introduction for middle managers to various approaches to diagnosing and solving problems with throughput. You can find other resources on his website, www.toc-goldratt.com.

Solving Throughput Problems

Once a source for the throughput problem has been identified, middle managers should focus their improvement efforts on finding the solution that will most improve results. For the best results and whenever possible, you should involve team members and peers in defining and implementing each solution. Involving others will improve commitment and accuracy, and will speed up the implementation of changes. Let's look at six of the most common types of solutions.

Solution 1: Distinguish Constraints from Bottlenecks

Middle managers may waste time removing bottlenecks that are not constraints. Individuals, teams, or departments who seek to optimize their part of a process without looking at the whole picture are most likely to face this problem. Here is a simple process with both the bottlenecks and the constraint identified.

In this process, steps B, C, D, and E are bottlenecks and step D is the constraint. Work will pile up waiting for steps B and C to be completed and a huge pileup will accumulate before step D. The people or machines doing step E will sit idle if not utilized in other processes or projects.

Until step D's performance improves, the overall process will produce at an approximate pace of 10. If this were a process contained within one team, it would be obvious that step D should be the starting point for improvement. But what if this process spanned several departments? In this case, you would need to work together to identify the constraint and concentrate on improving performance. This example is a simple one, but middle managers can look at and analyze any work process or project in the same way. Understanding both bottlenecks and the constraint will give you a better picture of the potential options for improving throughput. Using the process depicted in figure 8-7, for example, the following questions might come to mind:

- What actions will improve step D's performance?
- Is there another resource, person, system, or machine that can take over some of step D's workload?
- What can the other process steps do to make step D's job easier and more efficient?
- Can steps A, B, and E provide resources to another process to improve its throughput?
- What throughput pace is acceptable? How can the work flow be optimized to enable the team to produce consistently at this pace?

Middle managers who take the time to identify and understand bottlenecks and constraints will have a valuable tool for improving results. Focusing on constraint performance will ensure that time and resources have the highest benefit.

Figure 8-7. A Process with Four Bottlenecks and One Constraint

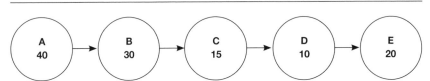

Solution 2: Reduce the Impact of Constraints

Once you identify a constraint, you can work to improve or supplement the constraint's performance. This is often the most valuable work that a middle manager can do, which makes this work a priority on the 80/20 list (the 20 percent of effort that produces 80 percent of the results). When dealing with constraints, consider using these steps:

1. *Test to ensure the proper identification of the constraint.* Constraints may be obvious or difficult to identify. To make sure that you identify the constraint correctly, ask yourself whether improving this process step would result in overall improvements to throughput. If the answer is yes, then it is more than likely that this resource is the constraint.

2. *Determine the potential capacity of the constraint.* The constraint capacity is the amount of work, related to a particular process, that can possibly be done under the best of circumstances. Middle managers need to be cautious not to consider a resource's total capacity when evaluating a constraint if the resource serves multiple processes or projects.

3. *Identify ways to improve capacity.* Is it always possible to improve the capacity of a resource? Sometimes yes, sometimes no. Simplification, automation, and upgrading abilities or skills are a few ways to improve the capacity of a resource.

4. *Identify additional resources to help lessen the constraint.* Sometimes a resource needs to be augmented to improve throughput. When the constraint is a person, you, as a middle manager, will want to look at delegating work away from the constraint and rebalancing the workload. When the constraint is a system step, augmenting performance means adding components or diverting work to another part of the process.

5. *Optimize the efficiency of the constraint through better setups and handoffs.* Middle managers may be able to improve the throughput of the constraint by changing the way work gets to and leaves this resource. If the process step preceding the constraint has excess capacity (relative to the pace of the constraint), then having it take extra time to better prepare the work going to the constraint will be time well spent. Can you or a team member more effectively organize, document, or communicate the work before it gets to the constraint? Can the upstream resource queue up the work more effectively? Is the slowest person or machine spending time doing work that people or machines before or after it can perform?

Solution 3: Reduce Bottlenecks When Necessary

In at least two situations, you as a middle manager will want to focus on reducing bottlenecks to throughput. First, you need to address bottlenecks that are likely to become the next constraint, especially if the current constraint is already a focus for improvement. Second, you will want to reduce bottlenecks as part of an overall process redesign or optimization. Improving bottleneck performance may allow it to augment the constraint's performance or become a resource for other processes. Here are some steps you can take:

1. *Test to ensure that improving this bottleneck will improve results.* Before you spend time and energy on improving the performance of a bottleneck, you should assess whether the effort will make enough of a difference to warrant investment. Will this improvement pass the 80/20 test?
2. *Determine the bottleneck's capacity.* How much high-quality work can this resource complete? Can this resource produce more?
3. *Identify ways to improve capacity.* Is the employee or process efficient? Are all elements of the work necessary? Is there an opportunity to automate or combine steps?
4. *Identify additional resources to decrease the effect of bottlenecks.* As they do when trying to improve constraint performance, middle managers should utilize other resources to help improve the overall performance of a process or project. Those who develop their skills in

workload balancing will find they have more choices for improving throughput.

5. *Optimize the efficiency of the bottleneck through better setups and handoffs.* It is important to ensure that work arrives at bottlenecks quickly and efficiently. If team members need to look up information or get an excessive number of approvals before beginning the work, their output will suffer. Bureaucracy and red tape often get in the way of progress, particularly when they affect a constraint or bottleneck.

Solution 4: Shorten Critical Paths

Many throughput problems occur because the process or project design does not support the needed pace of throughput. Middle managers often underestimate the time needed to get through the various parts of a process or critical path. Corky's hiring process was an example of this. She thought that candidates should be able to get through the hiring process in a week in addition to the two weeks' notice the candidate would need to give to his or her current employer—in other words, a total of 19 days. The critical path for the hiring process, however, took 24 days. Middle managers who take time to understand and improve the critical path of important work processes will be in a better position to improve their team's throughput and results. Here are some steps you can take when dealing with critical paths:

1. *Ensure that the critical path is accurate and complete; beware of hidden steps or delays!* When determining a critical path, managers should consider each component of the work, including smaller or shorter steps like approvals, paperwork, mailing times, and vendor lead times. It is also dangerous to assume the best-case scenario for estimating a critical path. Getting a signature on paperwork could happen in just a few minutes, but is this typical?

2. *Test assumptions about each step on the critical path.* If the critical path is unacceptably long, you, as a middle manager, can begin to shave time off by challenging the assumptions behind each step. Does the work need to take this long? Is every step necessary? Can process changes allow for more steps that are concurrent?

3. *Identify ways to shorten each step on the critical path.* Middle managers can make tasks more efficient by considering alternative ways of doing the work. Can team members transmit, communicate, and share information electronically? Which tasks are candidates for automation? Can team members reduce specific parts of the work and still produce high quality results?

4. *Identify ways to shorten handoff times.* The critical path length may double when it includes the time needed for handoffs. The handoff, or process connection, often does not add any value to the work other than to facilitate communication and understanding. Reducing handoff times can be a quick and easy way to improve throughput. To reduce process connection delays, middle managers must first define them and objectively determine their length or time. Managers can then reduce the number of process connections by challenging the use of each handoff. Eliminate needless handoffs. For cross-functional processes, it may be necessary to collaborate with peers to diagnose the root causes of slow process connections to seek alternative approaches.

5. *Reduce unnecessary steps.* Most processes, particularly everyday work processes, have unnecessary steps. Identifying and eliminating unnecessary steps is the "low hanging fruit" of process improvement. It is quick and effective, but it can only occur when middle managers analyze and evaluate work processes.

6. *Determine methods for doing more work concurrently, but ensure that doing so will improve throughput.* The more interdependent steps in the work process there are, the longer the critical path will be. To support an environment where team members can work on many tasks at the same time, middle managers must communicate the status and progress of the work often and fully.

Solution 5: Improve Skills

Training and development are useful managerial tools for improving throughput. Both you and your team members need to ensure that you have the skills needed to complete the work quickly and well. It can be difficult for middle managers to evaluate their own development needs, but it becomes easier when the focus is on results and throughput. Are you getting projects completed on time? Do you wish results were better? With what tasks do you struggle? Are you able to complete the analytical work needed to solve throughput problems? Are you able to plan well? The answers to these and other questions may help you determine new skills that could benefit your team:

1. *Objectively determine needed skills.* To maximize throughput, middle managers need to be excellent analyzers, planners, and communicators. The most common middle management development needs are in the areas of planning and organizing. These skills are also critical for improving throughput. Middle managers who struggle with deadlines and seem disorganized may need help and development in these areas. If your team members are unclear about their priorities and work assignments, then you definitely need training in planning and organizing. For team members, time management and problem identification are often skills that need improvement. Specific technical skills may also help the manager and his or her team members work more effectively.

2. *Identify teaching resources.* Who in the organization is strong in the area needing development? Can they mentor an employee needing development? What training options will work best in this case? Search for recent books, tapes, and articles on the topic. For middle managers who need to develop their ability to plan and analyze work, there are, unfortunately, fewer choices. Finding a mentor or coach within or outside the organization will probably be the best solution for developing these important skills.

3. *Establish learning follow-up and reinforcement.* Middle managers who take the time and energy to develop themselves and team members should also invest in follow-up and in reinforcing these newly developed skills. The best way to reinforce learning is to use the new skills! If team members have attended training, make sure they utilize the new skills they have learned. This will benefit the team and provide them with work that is likely to be intrinsically motivating.

Solution 6: Deal with Other Barriers to Throughput

Barriers to throughput regularly challenge middle managers. These general skills for diagnosing and solving problems will be invaluable tools for dealing with most of these challenges:

1. *Diagnose the root cause of problems affecting throughput.* Middle managers who ask why problems occur until they get to the root cause of an issue will be in a better position to effect real and lasting improvements. To diagnose the root causes of problems, excellent collaboration skills and a healthy sense of curiosity are important. Review each of the potential problems affecting throughput presented earlier in this chapter. Ask peers and team members for input. Test ideas and assumptions to determine if they are valid.

2. *Notice and address patterns, themes, and recurring barriers.* Many problems occur repeatedly but may go unnoticed for some time. Often, the only way to see and understand the problem is to take notice of and address patterns such as difficulty or recurring smaller issues. Is there a theme or pattern that could shed light on the underlying problem with a process or project?

3. *Become a barrier obliterator.* Middle managers who make it their mission to seek out and destroy barriers to throughput will improve results more quickly and completely than those who do not. Being proactive or reacting quickly is better than waiting until results deteriorate and the barriers no longer respond quickly to efforts at their removal. Middle managers lose precious time when they do not address emerging problems. High-impact managers often think about the things getting in the way of throughput and then they take action to improve results.

The Most Important Question Middle Managers Should Ask

Middle managers who want to improve throughput should always ask this question: "What are the one or two changes that will have the most impact on the overall throughput of this work?" Said another way the question becomes "What is the 20 percent that will improve throughput by 80 percent?" Whether the focus is on the constraints, bottlenecks, critical paths, connections, skills, mucky-muck, or other barriers, the question is the same. A few improvements can have a significant and positive impact on results. Middle managers should seek out and implement these value-added improvements as much as possible.

It is not always easy to discern the changes that will have a significant impact from those that will not make much of a difference. To ensure that you have determined the best changes to make, ensure that adequate analysis and testing have been done. In addition, the impact previous changes have made should be assessed and considered. Do not make the same or similar mistakes repeatedly. Once your team implements a modification, they should closely monitor throughput to evaluate the effect the change is having.

Using High-Impact Management to Make the Most of Your Busy Day

Jim felt discouraged about how little he was accomplishing at work. Every day was an exercise in frustration, playing catch-up, and rolling tasks onto tomorrow's to-do list. He always felt behind the curve—despite working extra hours. He was not able to prioritize his schedule because everything seemed important; and he spent most of his day in meetings or talking with his managers. He knew that the ways in which he spent his time did not match up with his manager's priorities and expectations for him, but he still allowed himself to gravitate toward doing the work that was most comfortable for him, rather than what needed to get done. Though he talked a great deal about the importance of planning, he spent more time talking about planning than actually doing it. He used planners, to-do lists, and white boards, but still felt that he was not on top of things. In addition, he stalled out when he was emotionally uncomfortable with a task or decision.

Jim is not alone. Many middle managers have more tasks on their to-do list than they can ever complete, and they don't know what they can do to improve their situation. They wish they had a clone, or two, to help knock off more work. This state of affairs is endemic to the job of middle management—especially busy public-sector managers—and is not something that will go away by working two more hours each day. Working more is not the answer, and burnout the likely result. To gain control of their day, middle managers should examine how they are spending time and make choices that will yield better results.

Five Fallacies about Time

One of the barriers middle managers face regarding their time is their perception of time management. How many times have you heard yourself, or a fellow middle manager, utter these statements:

- Time is precious.
- There is never enough time!
- If it ain't broke, don't fix it.
- If it is worth doing, it's worth doing right.
- Slowing down decreases output.

All five of these statements are fallacies about time. If you are a busy middle manager who works too much (many middle managers fit into this group), the best solution to issues with time might be to change your beliefs about time and your definition of what successful use of your time looks like. Let's look at the five fallacies about time, which illustrate how beliefs can get in the way of good time management.

Fallacy 1: Time Is Precious

Most people—in their hearts and minds—believe that time is precious. That said, if someone were to follow you around all day, would that person get the sense that you valued time? For many managers, what they intend (to use time wisely) and what they do (give time away like it is a cheap commodity) are completely different.

Voni was a smart, hardworking middle manager who led the race and social justice program. Although she worked long days and on weekends, she felt that she was making good choices about how she spent her time. When pressed by her boss to take on another project, she pushed back, saying that she and her team did not have time. When he suggested that she do a time audit to see where her time was going, she realized that she had been wasting nearly a third of her day on activities that were not critical to her program's success.

All managers schedule their time with the best of intentions, but it is easy to let meeting invitations, off-topic drive-by conversations, and FYI (for your information) email exchanges suck time away from more important tasks.

Fallacy 2: There Is Never Enough Time!

As managers get older and retire, they rarely think back and wish they had spent more time at the office. If anything, their sentiments are quite the opposite. Many managers lament that they lost important parts of their lives by working too much. Time is a unit of life, a slice of one's experience here on Earth. A middle manager has more than 10,000 minutes each week to divvy up for what's most meaningful, important, or fun to do. Those who regularly choose to work too many hours a week are shortchanging other parts of their lives.

As a middle manager, making good choices about how to manage your time is not just a desirable thing to do, it is essential. Like a traffic cop in the middle of a busy intersection, middle managers need to make good decisions about which work moves forward and how quickly.

Managers who work more will often produce less. This may sound counterintuitive, but managers who routinely work late or on weekends are not as productive or effective as those who spend fewer hours at work. Although you may work more than 60 hours a week, your number of truly productive hours is generally less than 40. At a certain point, the exhaustion of working 60 hours a week will yield diminishing returns in terms of loss of concentration, diminished creativity, and low morale. The way to become more successful is not to work harder but to work smarter.

Mindy was a middle manager who worked too much. She was invited to take part in numerous meetings about all aspects of the agency, and people valued her input and ideas. She liked to participate, enjoyed knowing what was going on in the agency, and had a hard time saying no. Because these meetings took up so much of her day, she worked evenings and weekends to get her other work done. She allowed herself to become the go-to person for more topics than was practical or efficient. She accepted, and sometimes encouraged, scope creep, which broadened her job responsibilities to the point that she could do many things halfheartedly but only few well.

Deep down, Mindy knew this and was worried about it to the point that it took a toll on her health. When she was under pressure, she was jittery, had a nervous tic, and did not take the time to listen during conversations. She was present in body, but her mind was absent. This only exasperated the problem. She used her busy schedule as an excuse for not managing better. Senior management could see she was busy and working long hours, and, as a result, let her poor performance slide. Over time, her managers' expectations of her fell. Her job performance suffered, and she did not achieve the best results possible. Her life was out of balance.

Jane's work style was different but no more effective. In addition to spreading herself too thin and getting involved in too many tasks, she puttered her time away. She worked numerous hours, but many of them were spent on unimportant tasks. She did not know how to prioritize, plan, or execute work, and she did nothing to ensure that her team was working on the right action plans. As a result, she and her department spent their time on tasks that made little difference within the agency.

Jane allowed herself to spend several hours a day responding to routine requests and inquiries. A better use of her time would have been to build up the independence and capacity of her organization, so that each of her team members would be able to address and solve many of their daily issues. She focused on the tyranny of the urgent rather than on what was valuable. She also procrastinated until the last possible moment, and then she came in evenings and on weekends to get her work done on time, or at least not too late. However, she never left enough time, so her work was often poorly done and incomplete. She had more than enough time to get her job done, but she wasted most of it.

Jim, Mindy, and Jane would probably all say that if they only had more time, they could be more successful. The fact was that even if they had more time, their poor time management habits would get in the way, and they would end up producing the same unsatisfactory results. They did not need more time; they needed to spend their time more productively. Until middle managers are using their 40 hours a week optimally, they should resist the temptation to work more hours and throw the rest of their life out of balance.

Fallacy 3: If It Ain't Broke, Don't Fix It

One of the greatest wastes of time is continuing to do things the same way because it seems to be working. Often, middle managers do not even know if their processes, systems, or practices are serving the outcome, because they have not recently evaluated them. Sticking with the status quo may not save time and is more likely to waste it. What if there were a better way to do the work? Have the conditions that justified the current approach changed? What if the goals have changed but the work has not?

As the primary change agent within your agency, you, as a middle manager, need to question the status quo and ensure that processes and practices are set up to deliver the desired results. When goals change, practices and processes must also change. Hesitating or failing to change ideas or approaches that are comfortable wastes time and money. (Techniques for improving processes can be found in chapter 7.)

Jake told his middle managers that he wanted them to improve their analysis capabilities so they could make better decisions. The end goal was to increase productivity, quality, and profitability throughout the organization. It was a great strategy, but it proved hard to achieve. Jake and many of the other middle managers assumed that the goal of greater accountability and ownership could happen using their current agency practices. They were wrong.

As things stood, many of their agency's processes and systems did not support the type of functional analysis and optimization that Jake and the other managers wanted to implement. Middle managers could not get the data they needed to make sound judgments. In addition, team members did not buy into the idea that they should spend more time measuring their effectiveness, nor did they know how to accomplish this. Their comfortableness with the status quo was getting in the way and wasting time. To improve results, they needed to question whether their current processes and systems were satisfactory or needed to be changed.

Fallacy 4: If It Is Worth Doing, It's Worth Doing Right

The problem with this statement comes from how middle managers define "doing things right." If the standard for "right" is perfect or restrictive, then waiting to do things right could lead to procrastination, inaction, and bottlenecks. Of course, high quality work is important and always the goal; but if you wait to do things until conditions are perfect, you will produce less and miss important opportunities.

Bob fell into this time trap a lot. He procrastinated because he wanted to wait until he had enough time to focus on the problem or opportunity. Guess what? He never had enough time—and was never going to. He missed several opportunities because he was simply too picky and slow. Why was he like this? It was because he felt that if he were not perfect, his customers would not value him. Though his internal and external customers wanted high-quality work, what they missed most from him and his team was action and results.

Lonny knew that several members of his team were not performing adequately. But each time his manager talked with him about this, he had another reason why the time was not right to make the necessary changes. The busy season was coming up, and he didn't have time to train new employees. His team had recently lost a member, so he couldn't afford to make any changes in personnel. There was a new supervisor on the team, and Lonny wanted to see if his employees might respond to this new person more favorably—and on and on. Each excuse may have been valid, but together they formed a pattern of inaction and demonstrated Lonny's hesitancy to take care of the problem. The conditions were never going to be perfect for him to take control of the situation and make the necessary changes. Eventually, he was fired and replaced by a manager who was willing to be more proactive.

If you're one of those middle managers who has the tendency to wait too long to take action, a good mantra might be Shakespeare's famous line "He who hesitates is lost." Waiting until the timing is just right wastes time and slows down progress.

Fallacy 5: Slowing Down Decreases Output

In some cases, going slow is the best way to go faster. Ready, aim, fire. Slow, slow, fast. To achieve excellent results, it is best to complete a methodical, up-front analysis (slow), plan well (slow), and energetically implement (fast). Middle managers who spend more time on up-front planning, building relationships, and ensuring that the work supports their goals will outpace and outperform those who rush things. In addition, pausing midstream to analyze how the work is going can create much-needed energy to move the work forward or facilitate a breakthrough.

At Black & Decker, one of the key factors that enabled the team to reduce the product development cycle for the DeWalt power tool line was investing more time up front. Black & Decker devoted more time to ensuring they knew the features and benefits each tool should have, and then to designing the tool for the highest quality and manufacturability. They also took time in the beginning to do some team training and role clarification, which improved productivity and communication during the project management phase. Because of the time allocated up front, they were able to shorten the product development cycle by months.

Be aware, however, that sometimes being slow is just taking too much time. The activities that take time up front but pay off in the end include good analysis, effective planning, clarifying expectations and roles, and relationship building. Middle managers who spend more time doing these things will find that their throughput improves.

Letting Go of the Victim Mentality

The five fallacies about time prevent middle managers from making the most of their day. Another significant barrier that reduces your effectiveness is "victim conversations" about time. A victim conversation is something you say or think that has a "woe is me" quality to it. When it comes to time, a victim conversation might sound like this:

I am so busy, I can't think straight.
I don't have time for this.
Another day is gone and I didn't put a dent into my to-do list.

Debbie was a big whiner when it came to time. Although she had a huge job and many time-related challenges, her victim conversations got in her way more than all her other challenges put together. Her victim conversations kept her from taking action and stopped her from thinking creatively. When she thought or spoke about her frustrations about time, in that moment, she made it impossible to progress. Think about how ridiculous these complaints sound:

> I can't believe the day is already half over. I have not spent five minutes at my desk all day. I do not know when I am going to be able to get this done. I would not wish this job on my enemy.

How can anything productive follow statements like these? When people like Debbie habitually gripe about not having enough time, they are sealing their fate and making their problem worse. Venting frustrations now and then is natural, but when it is a common response, the victim conversation becomes a major barrier to success.

High-Impact Management Techniques for Mastering Time

High-impact managers have beaten the time demons and learned to make wise choices about how to spend their day. They know that managing time well will enable them to work more on meaningful projects and establish the better work/life balance needed for them to stay sane and happy. The high-impact management techniques for mastering time include

- Perform periodic time audits.
- Set the pace.
- Apply the 80/20 rule to choices about time.
- Use tiny pockets of time to get big results.
- Plan, plan, plan.

In addition, these managers have come to know that their good time management habits have rubbed off on their team members. High-impact managers lead by example. Let's look at each of the five techniques listed just above.

Technique 1: Perform Periodic Time Audits

The best way for middle managers to determine how efficiently they use time is to complete a time audit. A time audit reveals the level of alignment that exists between the middle manager's goals and how he or she spends time. Unlike other time inventories, the time audit does not seek to detail how a manager spends each minute. The time audit focuses on the type of activity, not each specific action. Not only would it take too much time to complete a detailed inventory, it is also unnecessary. To perform a time audit, complete exercise 9-1.

The time audit emphasizes the things that are most important for a middle manager to devote his or her time to. Here are a few suggestions for each part of the time audit given in exercise 9-1.

Time Audit: Part 1

Part 1 is a place to establish what the priorities should be. It is important to take the time to fill out this part so the answers can be referred to during the other parts of the audit. In addition, the act of summarizing the priorities will help middle managers focus on them.

Time Audit: Part 2

Middle managers should spend at least 75 percent of their time, or six hours a day, on the work described in part 1. It is important to make sure the actions are not only aligned to goals, but that they are also the best choices from many possible actions. For example, asking a peer about a concern may support resolving the concern, but is this action going to make a difference? Would calling a meeting and brainstorming potential solutions be a better use of the same time?

Middle managers tend to spend too much time in meetings. It is valuable to question the meetings you attend and their effectiveness. If a meeting is not effective, ask the meeting leader to make positive changes; or stop attending, if possible.

Middle managers need to focus on enabling their employees to perform their best. Many busy middle managers allow their attention to get diverted by the needs of the day and may go months without thinking about how to coach and facilitate performance. Ideally, optimizing individual and team performance, as identified in part 1, is a top priority. If not, it should be added to the list.

It is also important for you to feel comfortable that your management peers and employees would agree that you are spending time in

Exercise 9-1. Perform a Time Audit

Part 1	Response
My broad goals, based on my manager's expectations, are . . .	
My most important priorities are . . .	
I am most concerned about . . .	
The barriers getting in the way of my team's productivity are . . .	
Planning and analysis that I need to complete in the next month . . .	
Part 2	**Response**
The approximate percentage of my time spent on items described in part 1 is . . .	
Are the actions I am taking adding value?	
The average number of hours a week I have spent in meetings is . . .	
Are these meetings a good use of my time? Why? / Why not?	
Which meetings should I keep and which should I no longer go to?	
Are the meetings well run and effective?	
How successful are my employees? What have I done to optimize their performance?	
How clear is my team about which tasks are of highest priority?	
If I shared how I spend my time with my manager, peers, and employees, what would they likely say?	
How much time over the last week did I spend doing versus managing?	
How many hours do I work on average?	
Part 3	**Response**
Based on this audit, what goals should I set to improve how I spend time?	
What beliefs should I take on to help support these goals?	
What immediate actions can I take to begin using my time more wisely?	

Note: A full-size version is available for download at www.lisahaneberg.com.

the ways that matter most. If you don't think they would agree with your choices, then expectations and priorities might need to be realigned and you might need to say "no" more often. Overall, middle managers should be able to gain support and agreement that they are working on the tasks that are most important and beneficial.

It is important to notice if doing gets more attention than managing, and why. If so, is it because doing is more comfortable and satisfying?

Middle managers who work more than 40 hours a week, on average, should look at how they spend their time and ensure that they get the most value out of each hour worked. Managers who work more than 60 hours a week are not managing their time well and should seek to reduce the number of hours worked while improving productivity.

Time Audit: Part 3

Beliefs that could help you manage your time might include statements like, "As a middle manager, I am expected to optimize individual and team performance, and I need to be spending more time focusing on this to meet this expectation and responsibility"; or "Right now the top priority is planning for the coming busy season. Time spent working on this now will benefit my team and me later. I need to make sure that nothing gets in the way of this important planning."

Be bold and assertive when making your list of immediate actions to take to improve time management, because doing so will be more energizing and empowering. "I don't know" is not an acceptable answer to this question. The list should contain at least 10 possible actions.

The time audit is useful for determining the alignment that exists between how a middle manager spends his or her time and the most important results. If you find you are spending too much time on tasks not listed in part 1 of the time audit, try to resist the urge to rationalize or make excuses. Though it is true that most middle managers face dozens of requests a day for their time, it is your responsibility to determine the best method to get the work completed. Middle managers need to be able to decline requests that get in the way of work that should be their top priority.

Technique 2: Set the Pace

Middle managers determine the pace of the organization. "Pace" is the rate at which work proceeds, but it is also the rate at which a person walks. For middle managers, both definitions are important. To establish and maintain an electric, exciting, and productive pace within which it feels good to work, the pace of the work and the people needs to be brisk. In a work environment like this, workers feel like making things happen and they accomplish more. In the for-profit world, Intel and Amazon.com are examples of companies with a brisk pace; there is nothing lethargic about their work environments! People walk down the hallways with determination and speed. They are clearly thinking about something. Within earshot are two people engaged in a lively discussion about how to solve a problem. In a meeting room, a manager is drawing a diagram on the white board, arrows going everywhere, heads nodding.

Although both Intel and Amazon.com are high-technology companies and might be expected to have a fast-paced environment, that is not why their work pace is fast. It is brisk because their middle managers make it so. Any workplace, even a federal agency or a 125-year-old paper mill, can have an exciting pace if the middle managers create that type of environment. Here's how to create pace:

- *Manage by walking around.* It does not do any good if you only leave your desk once a day. Managers who circulate and talk to their people, as well as those in other departments and their managers, are informed, perceived as accessible, and create a positive energy in the office.
- *Initiate action every day.* Get moving on projects or ideas that are on the to-do list. Do not allow procrastination to get in the way of action.
- *Facilitate meetings and ask people to participate* (as opposed to meetings where the leader speaks and everyone else just sits there). Facilitate brainstorming or problem-solving sessions on a regular basis.
- *Ask people for their ideas every day.*
- *Express a sense of urgency that comes from being excited about the work.*

- *Celebrate successes and create anticipation for future successes.*
- *Have fun at work.* Smile and laugh. Take the work seriously, but enjoy it too.
- *Make the removal of barriers and mucky-muck a top priority.* Don't let anything get in the way of your team's progress.

Tim, a middle manager leading the new green building initiatives team, was always on the move. Striding down the hallway, he looked like a man with a mission. But anyone could stop him and strike up a conversation. He would jump into the conversation with fervor and interest. He always worked at a brisk pace and emitted a focused energy that was contagious to others in his area. He would share at least one new idea daily. To his boss, Tim was a bit of a nuisance, but in a good way. His employees began thinking more quickly, too. Within three months, he had improved the pace of his new department by being an outstanding role model and encouraging a fun and lively work environment.

Technique 3: Apply the 80/20 Rule to Choices about Time

The time audit reveals whether or not you are spending your time on work that matters. As a middle manager, you can use the 80/20 rule to help make wise choices about how you use your time. Of all the items on an average daily to-do list, 20 percent are critical. This 20 percent produces 80 percent of the results. A high-impact manager identifies and focuses on this 20 percent. When the fire drills of the day begin to usurp time, high-impact managers prioritize the 20 percent of the work that needs to remain the focus. If something in the schedule must be cut, high-impact managers make sure that it's not part of this 20 percent.

Case Study

Jim's responsibilities were undergoing a fundamental shift. Jim and his manager had agreed that Jim's top priority was to leverage signs of recovery in the market and focus on maximizing revenue for the company. Jim's job was to make sure that the agency seized every available opportunity to increase revenues. Almost overnight, his focus changed. No longer would he spend time on any topic of discussion. He began entrusting his most competent managers with handling more issues and decisions without him. He

let his staff know that he was going to back out of selected meetings and spend more time focusing on tasks that were aligned with
his new mandate. His direct and forthcoming approach worked. His
managers quickly adjusted to the level and type of involvement that
were being asked of them. He learned that the best way to improve
how he spent his time was to first make different and better choices,
then clearly and openly communicate these changes to team members and peers. To keep himself on track, he would ask himself if the
task he was working on was going to have an impact on revenue. If
not, he would delegate the task to focus his time on his most critical
objective: generating revenue.

Sometimes middle managers think that if they work harder, they will
be able to accomplish their goals. Often, however, the most important
choice they make is about *what* they will do, not how hard they will work.
This point is illustrated in a short parable written by Ralph Stayer:

> I'm sitting in a quiet room at the Millcroft Inn, a peaceful little
> place hidden back among the pine trees about an hour out of
> Toronto. It's just past noon, late July, and I'm listening to the
> desperate sounds of a life or death struggle going on a few feet
> away.
>
> There's a small fly burning out the last of its short life's ener-
> gies in a futile attempt to fly through the glass of the windowpane.
> The whining wings tell the poignant story of the fly's strategy—
> try harder.
>
> But it's not working.
>
> The frenzied effort offers no hope for survival. Ironically, the
> struggle is part of the trap. It is impossible for the fly to try hard
> enough to succeed at breaking through the glass. Nevertheless,
> this little insect has staked its life on reaching its goal through raw
> effort and determination.
>
> The fly is doomed. It will die there on the windowsill.
>
> Across the room, ten steps away, the door is open. Ten sec-
> onds of flying time and this small creature could reach the out-
> side world it seeks. With only a fraction of the effort now being

wasted, it could be free of this self-imposed trap. The break-through possibility is there. It would be so easy.

Why doesn't the fly try another approach, something dramatically different? How did it get so locked in on the idea that this particular route and determined effort offer the most promise for success? What logic is there in continuing until death, to seek a breakthrough with "more of the same"? No doubt, this approach makes sense to the fly. Regrettably, it's an idea that will kill.

Trying harder and harder is an approach that makes sense to many middle managers. Unfortunately, it often leads to burnout rather than success. Trying harder isn't necessarily the way to achieve more. It may not offer any real promise for getting what you want out of life. Sometimes, in fact, it's a big part of the problem. If you stake your hopes for a breakthrough on trying harder than ever, you may kill your chances for success.

Creating Work/Life Balance

In his best-selling book *Maverick: The Success Story Behind the World's Most Unusual Workplace*, Ricardo Semler, the well-known and highly regarded CEO of Semco in Brazil, had this to say about the importance of handling time: "I took sixteen aspirins in just one day. Before I could reorganize Semco, I had to reorganize myself. Long hours were the first issue I tackled. They were one of the biggest symptoms of time sickness, a disease that afflicts far too many executives. So I set 7 p.m. as the time I would leave the office, no matter what. After that, I would go to the movies, read books (but not business books)—anything but work. I wouldn't do any work on the weekends, either.... Yes, I would attack my problem directly, and that problem was not simply the management of a business but something even more fundamental: the management of time."

Many managers suffer from what Semler calls time sickness. They equate quality with quantity and attack work backlogs with a try-harder mentality. This approach is a recipe for burnout and failure. High-impact managers have learned that managing time enables many other successes to occur.

Technique 4: Use Tiny Pockets of Time to Get Big Results

It is 8:53 a.m. and there is a meeting scheduled to begin at 9:00 a.m. Brett has prepared for the meeting, and the needed materials have been copied and organized and ready to distribute. What should he do now? There isn't enough time to start anything new—or is there? Glancing quickly at his to-do list, he gets up and seeks out one of his employees. He asks a few questions, clarifies what needs to occur, and asks the employee to follow up with peers in another department. Returning to his desk, he grabs his materials and several other items to drop off in the mailroom on the way to the meeting. In the hall outside the meeting, he chats with a peer and resolves an open issue on his to-do list. He quickly lets his employees know that they can immediately act on the information instead of waiting until the meeting is over. He is still among the first to arrive at the meeting, and in seven minutes, has accomplished three tasks that will help his team members work more effectively.

High-impact managers routinely use tiny pockets of time to accomplish tasks on their to-do lists. It's all too easy to waste the few minutes before meetings or appointments. Most people figure there is not enough time to start anything big, so why bother? There are two reasons that using these small amounts of time wisely will pay off. First, and most obviously, middle managers who use this time wisely will get more work done. If the average middle manager has five segments in their day, and the manager completes a couple of tasks before each segment begins, that's 10 additional tasks completed each day! Second, and just as important, doing things in these small bits of time energizes you and keeps you on pace. Conversely, wasting time scatters motivation and energy. Tasks that lend themselves to this practice include

- checking in with an employee
- asking a peer for clarification
- reading a quick article or memo
- sharing information
- requesting a report or information for analysis to be done later
- returning a phone call

- filling out paperwork that has been sitting in your in-box for too long
- sending out a meeting appointment and creating the agenda
- managing by walking around.

Middle managers can use tiny pockets of time to facilitate a breakthrough. Taking 10 minutes to ask new, open-ended questions can spur fresh thinking about how to solve an old problem. It takes just a few moments to create and deliver several new questions verbally or by email. If the questions help move the problem or project forward, these 10 minutes may prove to be the most valuable time you spend all day.

Technique 5: Plan, Plan, Plan

Most middle managers do not spend enough time planning. Often, they opt to deal with the tyranny of the urgent and let planning slide. This strategy is rarely effective, because it begins a vicious cycle of not spending time on the right tasks, because there is no good work plan, because there is no time to plan, and so on. Each day, middle managers should take a few minutes to plan their day. Weekly and monthly planning is equally as important. (Techniques for creating excellent work plans can be found in chapter 7.)

Planning can be a therapeutic practice for middle managers who worry that there is too much to do. Concerns about remembering what is most important and what might happen if something falls through the cracks are allayed when a good plan is in place. With a good work plan, you can breathe easier, because the most important work will be at the top of the list. Even though a work plan may be daunting and contain a long list of tasks, having a plan is always more comforting than worrying about "what-if" scenarios.

Middle managers who do not make good choices about how to spend their time will likely suffer from career setbacks, a poor work/life balance, and suboptimal results. To the casual observer, they may appear scattered and overwhelmed. Conversely, those who ensure their time is focused on doing the right things in an efficient manner will experience more success and satisfaction. They will appear to be on top of things and confident. High-impact managers have time to get their jobs done and be accessible and responsive to team members and peers. These effective managers periodically review how they are spending their time and ensure that they have their priorities straight. For the busy middle manager, time is a precious commodity that needs to be proactively and effectively utilized.

Case Study

Todd was an excellent planner. Fortunately, this skill rubbed off on his peers. In work sessions or meetings, he would frequently ask "What's the plan?" or "Do we have a plan for how we are going to accomplish this?" He would ask questions that slowed the group down and made them focus on the tasks involved, each person's role in the project, and due dates. This process prevented Todd and his team from overcommitting. He knew that taking the time to talk through the planning for each major project would serve him and his colleagues well in the end. His excellent planning helped them execute tasks more effectively. His work was never late. He managed his day to ensure that he completed the most important work first. When he committed to do something, people knew they could count on him to deliver.

Coaching: Helping Others Achieve Breakthroughs

One of the quickest and most effective ways for you to make an impact on your organization is through coaching. Coaching yields short-term and long-term payoffs. Helping others achieve breakthroughs boosts results today and builds the organization's skills for tomorrow. Unfortunately, coaching is an underutilized and poorly understood middle management tool. Many managers confuse coaching with advice and counseling. Figure 10-1 shows the similarities and differences among these three forms of influence. In the figure, the areas where the circles intersect represent shared characteristics:

- The impetus for all three methods is to help the other person. Those who offer advice mean well, even though their opinions may be unwelcome.
- Both advice and counseling are directive and quick, but the receiver may welcome neither.
- Both advice and coaching address less urgent concerns and may consider the receiver's ideas.
- Both counseling and coaching focus on goals and may be effective for changing long-term behavior.

- Each method is useful in certain circumstances. Coaching is the only method of influence driven by the receiver, and it is the most valuable way to improve his or her effectiveness and success.

Coaching is different from advising, preaching, counseling, and persuading, because the last four are all done from the viewpoint of and for the person offering it. Coaching is the exact opposite. A great coach talks little, listens a lot, and facilitates the thinking process of the receiver. When coaching, the focus is on the receiver's goals and possibilities, not the receiver's performance.

Figure 10-1. Three Ways to Influence Others

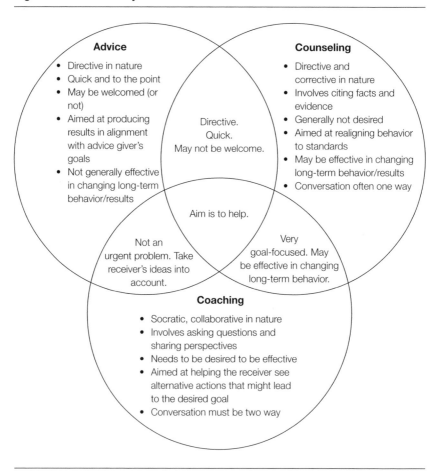

Coaches offer their time to help the progress of another. Coaches never try to replace the receiver's goals with their own (this would become advice or counseling). Though coaching is altruistic, it also benefits the middle managers who use it, because it improves results. It is important to recognize both the altruistic and selfish aspects of coaching because doing so will help you choose coaching techniques that are most helpful to the receiver and the organization.

Intrinsic motivation drives the best coaches to help others learn, grow, and perform. They get a charge out of helping people consider different viewpoints, and they enjoy seeing the proverbial light bulb turn on for them. Coaching can be one of the most fulfilling and meaningful roles for a middle manager. By helping others move their work forward, you broaden your reach within, and impact on, the organization.

Being a coach is rewarding—but not always easy. Sometimes the coach needs to be willing to discuss undiscussables or help uncover unwritten rules getting in the receiver's way. Receivers may perceive things in a way that is detrimental to their success. Coaches help them clarify what's real and what's not. A coach needs to be tough to hold the receiver accountable for realizing his or her goals. Doing this in a way that does not come across as bossy or directive can be tricky, but great coaches know that the secret lies in their intent to help, not control.

High-impact managers have a genuine interest in knowing how to help employees and peers be successful. They have learned techniques for facilitating helpful conversations. They know that coaching must be voluntary and welcomed by the receiver, not forced. Forced coaching becomes advice or feedback. Receivers should do most of the talking during coaching conversations. Great coaches ask many questions but otherwise let the receiver talk about their goals, ideas, and setbacks. They know that it is through this dialogue that the receiver is likely to see his or her challenge in a new and helpful way. Many people are comfortable with and welcome direction from their manager. Do not prescribe answers because this will prevent learning from taking place. (You can, of course, help them learn where to go to get the answers!)

High-impact management coaching helps middle managers and receivers get the most out of coaching discussions. The elements of high-impact management coaching are

- ad hoc coaching
- formal coaching conversations
- coaching with the use of Socratic questions
- coaching infrastructures.

Let's look at each element.

Ad Hoc Coaching

Todd walked into Lou's office and asked for a few minutes to chat. Todd had an open position in his department, and he knew that it was going to be hard to fill. The tasks were so specific to the agency that a current employee would best fill the job. Unfortunately, Todd could not think of a qualified internal candidate. Their conversation went like this:

LOU: What skills and behaviors are you looking for?

TODD: This position requires analytical skills, knowledge of the business, a proactive leadership presence, and—

LOU: Do they really need to be strong in all of these areas? Do other members of the team have experience in these areas?

TODD: The other team members are strong, yes, and they have worked for the company for a long time. So the new person does not need to have it all.

LOU: Which skills are the most important? What about filling this position concerns you most?

TODD: Above all else, I need someone who is a self-starter and who will take charge of the function. What I fear most is not being able to drive improvements fast enough.

LOU: If this is the case, why does the person need to come from inside the company?

TODD: I guess they don't, but I would prefer it.

LOU: OK, but keep challenging yourself on that assumption. Are there other positions that require similar skills and experiences?

TODD: There are a few I can think of.

LOU: Do any of the individuals in these positions have the behavioral qualities important for this job?

TODD: I'm not sure.

LOU: Are there employees in the operations group that have these skills?

TODD: I don't know. I would not have thought of them. Perhaps there are.

LOU: Do you know of any managers whose strengths may not be a match to their current position?

TODD: Yes, there are a few people like that…hmmm. Wait a minute; I've got it. Thanks. I will talk to you later!

Ad hoc coaching can occur anytime and in various ways. A breakthrough can occur while chatting in the hallway. High-impact managers seize opportunities to help their employees and peers. The dialogue between Todd and Lou is an example of ad hoc coaching. Middle managers practice ad hoc coaching when they take the initiative to ask questions that invigorate another person's thinking. Lou made it a habit to arrive a few minutes early to meetings. During this time, those around the table engaged in small talk and shared what was on the top of their minds. Lou had a knack for asking just the right question to help someone think about his or her problem in a new way. Lou would follow up with the employee after the meeting if it seemed that it would be helpful. Peers often shared their frustrations about projects they were struggling with, and Lou would offer to help them brainstorm and organize their thoughts.

Many managers think they coach more than they actually do. In reality, however, giving advice is a far more common practice than coaching. The primary distinction between ad hoc coaching and advice is the number of open-ended questions that typifies coaching. In addition, a good coach will resist the urge to tell people what they should do. Techniques for providing excellent ad hoc coaching include

- Be available and accessible. Ad hoc coaching can only occur if both parties have the time to talk. Middle managers who leave no time for informal discussions or who frequently close their office door will miss out on many opportunities to coach. Arrive at meetings a few minutes early, eat in the lunchroom, periodically have lunch with peers and employees, and stroll through the office several times a day.
- Listen. Employees and peers will share what is on their minds and highest on their list of challenges and concerns. Pick up on conversations in meetings and casual conversations.
- Use Socratic questions to draw out new information and ideas (see the examples later in this chapter). Express genuine interest and curiosity.
- Facilitate action plans. Receivers may have a difficult time putting their ideas and thoughts into an organized action plan. Coaches can help the receiver take action by making it easier for him or her to get started.
- Encourage. The receiver may be looking for someone to say, "Go for it!" Coaches encourage others to try new approaches and stretch boundaries.

Ad hoc coaching is a fantastic way for you to enable your team members to achieve results. Coaches who keep their eyes open and reserve their opinions will find ample opportunities to provide coaching and make a difference.

Formal Coaching Conversations

Ad hoc coaching works for many people and situations, but not all. Sometimes the best approach is to set aside time for a more formal coaching conversation. These formal conversations are most suitable for enabling large projects or personal goals to get off the ground. The primary reason for scheduling a formal session is to ensure that enough time is set aside to have a fruitful discussion. The coaching conversation will be more effective when the coach and receiver embrace appropriate roles, as follows.

The coach:

- Asks the receiver to define his or her goal. What is he or she hoping to make happen?
- Keeps the discussion on track and moving.
- Asks questions that stimulate discussion (see the section on Socratic questions later in this chapter).
- Summarizes and clarifies discussion topics.
- Clarifies understanding of the receiver's goals and his or her motives for having those goals.
- Helps the receiver develop an action plan.
- Facilitates small victories for the receiver. For example, Lou knew that Denny wanted to learn more about other parts of the agency and arranged for him to participate on a cross-functional project team. This assignment exposed him to several other functional groups and benefited the overall organization.

The coaching conversation progresses as the coach asks questions and makes statements that help to further the receiver's thinking. The goal for this discussion is for the receiver to expand his or her viewpoint, generate new approaches to meeting goals, and to dispel assumptions or beliefs that are getting in the way of progress. The receiver may change his or her goals based on new insights or information. When done well, the receiver leaves the coaching session energized with new ideas and a clearer focus.

The receiver:

- Shares his or her goal, desired outcome, ideas, and motivations for the goal.
- Discusses questions, frustrations, and problems he or she has already faced.
- Shares the information that he or she has collected thus far.
- Defines his or her basic interpretations, judgments, assumptions, and points of view.

- Reviews the current progress he or she is making toward the goal and defines the barriers that are getting in the way.
- Is open to exploring new ideas and approaches.

Using Socratic Questions

Middle managers who use Socratic questions collect useful information that helps them coach and lead their functions. As coaches, middle managers can help their employees and peers develop critical thinking and creativity skills. Socratic questions enable coaches to facilitate conversations in a more effective way.

The Socratic method, named for the Greek philosopher Socrates, emphasizes the use of thought-provoking questions to promote learning (instead of offering opinions and advice) and challenges widely held beliefs.

Socratic questions are probing and open ended. You can use these questions in a work context to help others develop. The inquiry process is the cornerstone of this practice, because it helps receivers think creatively and solve problems using new approaches. Socratic questions also help the receiver clarify what he or she understands and what is yet unknown. Through this inquiry, strategies for improving effectiveness emerge while energizing the receiver's curiosity. Middle managers who use Socratic questions challenge the receiver in a way that is intrinsically motivating. Let's look at several examples of Socratic questions.

Questions that clarify the receiver's goals:

- What would you like to have happen?
- How would you like to see this happen?
- Why are you favoring a change?
- What would you like to see change?
- If everything goes well, what will it look like in _____ months/years?
- In your mind, what will happen if we do not change?

Questions that clarify the receiver's intent or motives:

- Why do you want this?
- Why do you say that?

- How would you benefit?
- Why is this important?
- What made you think of this?
- Who benefits from this?

Questions to ensure that the receiver's goals are aligned to get results:

- How does this relate to your goal or objective?
- Where do you think this goal will lead?
- What does this mean?
- What do we already know about ...?
- Why is this your goal?
- What do you think will happen?

Questions to uncover the receiver's basic assumptions:

- What basic assumptions do you have about this?
- Are there other assumptions that could also be valid?
- How do you know that what you believe is true?
- Do you agree with the following assumption: ____? Why? / Why not?
- What does ____ think about this situation?
- What would happen if ...?
- What are the consequences of that assumption?
- Why do you think I asked this question?
- What is it about the question that is difficult to answer?

Questions to discover if the receiver has enough information:

- What do you need to know about this?
- What generalizations can you make?
- What data have you looked at already?
- How do you know that ____?
- Why do you think this is occurring?
- How can you be sure?
- Have you seen a situation like this before?
- What do you think is the cause?
- What evidence is there to support your assertion?

Questions to facilitate seeing other points of view:

- What would be an alternative?
- Is there another way to look at this? Why is it better?
- What are the pros and cons of this approach?
- How is this similar or different from what you have done in the past?
- What is the counterargument?
- What would someone who is against this idea say?
- What other ideas have you explored?
- How does this affect _____?

Socratic questions improve the coach's ability to remain objective by directing responses and conclusions back to the receiver. They also ask the receiver to consider many facets of a problem or goal, increasing the chances that new learning will occur.

Coaching Infrastructures

As a middle manager, you should think about how coaching can best be delivered in your organization. Some organizations, like Verizon and Intel, have utilized formalized coaching structures. Coaches are trained, assigned, and expected to meet at regular and ad hoc times. Often, these coaching structures also document goals and one's progress in reaching them. Intel's mentoring program uses the company intranet to match partners (the learners) with potential mentors. Mentors and partners work toward goals stated in their mentoring contract. Meeting frequency and design are then left up to the mentor and partner.

Former CEO Raymond Smith described coaching at Bell Atlantic (now Verizon) as an important part of their management culture:

> Coaching is not seen as the least bit corny or unusual in our agency. Once a week, one of us will ask, "Can I coach you on something?" In the past, I have never been able to do that comfortably. I was never able to do it without it being unnecessarily evasive on the one hand or unpleasant on the other. Now the

process is acceptable. It is group sanctioned. It's the way we've decided we're going to work together.

The pros of a formalized coaching structure include

- Coaching becomes part of the culture of the business.
- Assignment of coaches removes the stigma and embarrassment that some may associate with coaching.
- More people give and receive coaching under a formalized system.

The cons of a formalized coaching structure include

- Under a formalized coaching structure, the chances increase that people participate because it is compulsory or a corporate sacred cow. Mandatory systems often diminish some of the intrinsic motivation that can be associated with coaching.
- Formalized systems can be resource intensive and costly.
- Many formalized systems may not be flexible enough to meet the different needs of a diverse management group. It's hard to please all the people all of the time.

Many organizations, like Mead Paper and Amazon.com, do not utilize formalized coaching structures. In these types of organizations, coaching is encouraged and supported, but there are no formal training or expectations. (Organizations often say that managers should coach their employees, but most are not really talking about coaching as it has been defined here.) Most organizations fall into this category. At Amazon .com, dynamic small team groups are utilized to encourage learning and development. Their formula is to hire diverse and smart people and let coaching and knowledge transfer happen by osmosis. This model can work if the environment is set up to encourage team problem solving and idea generation.

The pros of an informal coaching structure include

- Coaching tends to be timely and need based.
- Those who are excellent coaches will likely coach more than those who are poor coaches. In other words, the spontaneous

and personal nature of the system will lead to certain people being sought out to coach more than others are—a natural selection, of sorts, for coaching.

■ Coaching and being coached are likely to be more intrinsically motivating when they are not compulsory.

The cons of an informal coaching structure include

■ Fewer people receive coaching and often the people who need it most do not seek out coaching.

■ Coaches are less likely to receive valuable training.

■ Without a structure to establish coaching as an important management tool, it is less likely to be valued and given a high priority.

In addition to formal and informal coaching structures, there are coaching models that fit along the spectrum between these two. There is no right or wrong method or approach to how coaching will be offered in an organization. As a middle manager, you are in the best position to assess and understand the best way to utilize coaching to develop people. Work with your peers, manager, and training department to ensure that the appropriate coaching model is evaluated and implemented. Why go to these lengths? Coaching, if done well, is one of your most powerful management tools. High-impact managers have learned that coaching and being coached is a high-value-added activity that enables you and your team members to achieve results.

Effective coaching helps you to maximize your impact. As a middle manager, you can help your staff achieve breakthroughs by recognizing and utilizing daily coaching opportunities. To be a great coach, it is first important to recognize what coaching is and what it is not. Giving someone your advice is not coaching. Whether you coach in an ad hoc or formal conversation, or as part of an established coaching structure, it is paramount that the coaching conversations be focused on and driven by the learner. By using these suggestions, you will improve your ability to coach peers and employees.

Coachability: How to Reach Goals Faster and Better

High-impact managers need to be highly coachable. What does being coachable mean? Much of a middle manager's day is concerned with guiding others, coaching team members, and assisting peers. However, it is just as important that middle managers ensure that they are getting the coaching, input, and development they need to be successful and continue to grow in their position. Coachability, then, is the degree to which you are open to what your environment can offer, or the extent to which you will accept and consider input and ideas.

High-impact managers know that their success depends on their being highly coachable when it counts most. Although all managers will be coachable some of the time and uncoachable during other moments, the most effective middle managers will be more coachable overall and, most important, during the times when it can make the greatest difference.

What Coachability Looks Like

Coachability is measured by how well a manager interacts with his or her environment; therefore, it is visible and observable behavior. Coachability is easy to recognize in others. When a manager is being coachable, there is an open, curious, and relaxed quality to his or her demeanor. When a manager is highly coachable, he or she:

- Is not defensive when challenged or offered an alternative view.
- Welcomes feedback and ideas for improvement.
- Asks for coaching.
- Considers and uses ideas offered by others.
- Seeks training and development in the form of reading, classes, new assignments, and coaching from others.
- Has a good sense of his or her strengths and weaknesses.
- Handles failures and setbacks with grace.

Being coachable usually goes hand in hand with confidence and a positive impression of one's own skills and abilities. Coachable managers display a sense of calm and a focus that allows them to take ideas and process them without feeling the need to defend or rationalize current methods. Highly coachable managers genuinely welcome and accept alternative points of view.

Middle managers who are uncoachable are also easy to identify. They put up barriers between themselves and others. Those who are uncoachable often look like this:

- They don't listen to ideas offered by others.
- They staunchly defend current ideas and approaches.
- They believe they must do things on their own and that asking for input is a sign of weakness.
- They appear to be unreceptive or not interested in coaching.
- They do not engage in conversations about development with their manager and view suggestions that they should develop new skills as criticism.
- They can be dismissive of others.

By observing how your peers behave during meetings and work sessions, you can begin to notice the behavioral cues that signal whether they are coachable or not. You should also seek to recognize these behaviors in yourself! Recognizing when you are being uncoachable is an important step toward improving your ability to accept constructive criticism.

Coachability Is a State of Mind

It is important to emphasize that people are not inherently coachable or uncoachable. Everyone has moments when they are coachable and others when they are not. Saying that someone is not a coachable person unfairly classifies him or her and does not recognize that coachability is a way of being that can be chosen at any given moment.

Middle managers interested in increasing their coachability need to examine what triggers their uncoachable moments. By understanding your personal triggers, you can recognize them and choose to be more coachable when the opportunity presents itself in the future. Here are examples of various emotional triggers:

- People triggered Harry's uncoachability when they questioned his decisions or opinions in front of his managers. He had a strong need to be right; and when challenged, he became uncoachable.
- Kathy refused to hear feedback if the idea suggested change or altered her tidy existence. She took great pride in planning her work; and when an idea had the potential to turn her world upside down, she resisted it, regardless of its merit or potential.
- Jim was often uncoachable when overwhelmed with too many tasks. His peers and managers eventually learned that it was best to save ideas or suggestions for another day if Jim had a backlog of projects or meetings.
- Corky was coachable when talking with others in her field of expertise but quickly became defensive about suggestions offered from individuals outside her department.

All middle managers encounter circumstances or people that trigger their uncoachability. Understanding and recognizing the obstacles that get in the way of your coachability is the first step toward becoming more receptive and, therefore, more successful. For example, a trigger for uncoachability may be something as simple as the time of day. You may find that you, or a peer, are not receptive to coaching at the end of a busy day that has been filled with meetings and projects. If you are sensitive about getting feedback or constructive criticism, you may prefer to schedule coaching sessions early in the morning before the majority of staff arrives or after most people have left the office and you are free of distractions. The size and composition of the group might also make a difference in how open you are to coaching. Do you prefer coaching sessions to be one-to-one, or with immediate peers? Are you less receptive to coaching if senior managers are present?

Even high-impact managers are human. It is important for you to be aware of your mood and recognize when you are not feeling coachable. It is better to reschedule a conversation or meeting for another time than to be uncoachable and get little from the conversation. Once you become aware of your triggers or resistance points, you can open yourself up to more opportunities for improvement and perhaps a breakthrough.

Coachability as a Definition of Success

High-impact managers strive to be extremely teachable. They adopt the belief that being highly coachable is important if they are to be successful. Coachable managers have altered their definition of what respect and competence look like. They know that they will be well regarded and held in higher esteem if they openly accept ideas and suggestions from others.

How Dell Encourages Coachability

Given that survival in the high-technology field is incumbent upon staying ahead of the knowledge curve, Michael Dell, the CEO of Dell Computer Corporation, cites coachability as a key requirement for himself, as well as the managers in his company. In his best-selling book *Direct from Dell: Strategies That Revolutionized an Industry*, Dell had this to say about learning:

> Our people are obviously motivated by the ways we link our goals to their compensation and incentives. But more importantly, there are ways in which we work to instill ownership thinking in our people and better leverage their talents so they can reach their full potential. The willingness and ability to learn constantly is one of them.... I approach learning from the standpoint of asking questions: What would make your job at Dell easier? What do our customers like and not like? What

would they like to see us doing better? How can we improve? I start by asking a lot of questions and doing a lot of listening: You don't learn anything when you're talking.

Stimulating, open, and meaningful conversations encourage coachability and learning. Middle managers who employ Dell's method of asking numerous open-ended questions will find that the coachability of others improves. The discussions that come out of such a dialogue will yield creative and useful ideas.

High-impact managers know that they will be much more successful if they focus on getting the best results, which will come from hearing and using the advice of many, rather than from being right. They regularly ask for input and coaching from many different people.

Techniques for Improving Your Coachability

In addition to recognizing when you are being coachable or uncoachable and embracing the belief that being coachable is important for success, there are several specific techniques you can use to improve your coachability. These methods will also help high-impact managers improve their ability to solve problems and generate creative opportunities. They include

- Coachability starts with a mindset. When you notice that you are being uncoachable, pause, take a deep breath, and decide to let go of the feelings of resistance and be more open.
- Ask more open-ended questions to glean more information about projects and processes.
- Ask follow-up questions to understand ideas and suggestions fully.
- Take the initiative to ask for input on one problem, idea, or topic each day.
- Resist the urge to defend yourself or say why an idea won't work. Focus on the desired outcome, not on being right.
- Schedule brainstorming and problem-solving meetings during the time of day or week that you are most coachable.

These techniques can help you immediately improve your overall coachability and ensure that you are being coachable when it matters most. High-impact managers have developed the ability to monitor their coachability and quickly choose behaviors that support that. They have learned that becoming more coachable is a test of mind over matter that gets easier with practice and experience.

Using Coachability to Attract a Breakthrough

Breakthroughs happen when people let them. Sometimes middle managers are like sponges, happily soaking in new information. All too often, however, preconceived notions, fears, and the ego shut out the opportunities that these managers seek. Coachability is the level of openness a manager has toward outside influences and development. There is a strong positive relationship between breakthroughs and a high level of coachability. Middle managers who want to experience breakthrough results can improve their odds by carefully preparing their work environment and themselves. To attract a breakthrough, try these 10 methods:

1. Let peers, managers, and employees know about the most important or interesting topics or challenges that you are working on. The more people are enrolled in a challenge, the better the chances that a terrific idea or approach will surface.
2. Call a meeting to brainstorm ideas and suggestions. Encourage diverse points of view and a variety of ideas. Go beyond inviting the most logical choices of people to the meeting and include those who have had great ideas about other problems.
3. Seek nontraditional avenues of information and ideas. Read current research and periodicals related to this topic.
4. Don't be shy. Call or email top thinkers and researchers in the field and ask for their perspectives.
5. Focus on defining the ideal desired outcome and asking questions about what conditions would need to exist to support this outcome.
6. Take, and be fully engaged in, a course on the subject.

7. Make a request that you would normally consider an unreasonable one. It generally does not hurt to ask, and may even work! Most middle managers are so conservative about what they ask for that their unreasonable requests are not likely to be that unreasonable.

8. Adopt a "this shall be" mindset. There seems to be some legitimacy to the self-fulfilling prophecy (when an expectation appears to lead to or cause the anticipated outcome), so managers might as well have this phenomenon work in their favor.

9. If important enough, ask an outside facilitator to lead a group of people through a work session to brainstorm ideas, approaches, barriers, and desired outcomes. Professional facilitators can often detect the dynamics of the group and guide the discussion for the best outcome.

10. Benchmark other admired and respected organizations that perform this particular task or process extremely well.

Breakthroughs are improvements that lead to a significant change. This change can be physically tangible, such as a new process or product, or in your mind, such as a new way of looking at an old problem. Either way, you can increase your odds of experiencing a breakthrough by taking the initiative to establish an environment that will support breakthrough thinking.

Coachability Opens Doors

Middle managers who increase their number of coachable moments will find the door of opportunity opens wide. Possibilities never thought possible become real, and obstacles fall by the wayside. Highly coachable middle managers are also highly promotable! Senior managers respect and value managers who do whatever it takes to produce the best results. Coachable managers will get more done and will utilize and implement more creative solutions than their peers who are less coachable.

Some middle managers do not value coachability because they believe that they need to appear strong and confident. Do not confuse confidence with ego. High-impact managers are strong, confident leaders and they are highly coachable. When middle managers can demonstrate both confidence and coachability, they improve their ability to get results through cooperation with other people and enjoy a successful career with many new and interesting challenges.

Coachability is an important qualification for high-impact managers. Middle managers need to be coachable to meet the diverse and challenging requirements of their jobs. By recognizing what coachability looks like and by employing techniques that enhance your coachability, you can improve your results and effectiveness. Being coachable is having a very engaged and interested state of mind—a feeling many find intrinsically motivating. Moving fast in the right direction feels great. Increased success and respect are great tonics that will reinforce the benefits of being coachable.

The High-Impact Management System: Putting It Together for Maximum Managerial Flow

As was described on the first page of the introduction, high-impact management has a rhythm, or a flow, that can be intensely satisfying and successful. In his book *Beyond Boredom and Anxiety*, Mihaly Csikszentmihalyi described the flow experience as one where moments flow in a unified, focused, and intrinsically stimulating manner. High-impact managers often experience flow at work. They are talented, prepared, and energized to make things happen. They have internalized their role and the beliefs that will serve them best. These managers have tried and now habitually practice most of the techniques presented in this book.

Reread the first two paragraphs of the introduction. Here they are again:

> In any organization, there are two kinds of middle managers. There are those who get the work done but never think beyond what needs to be completed in the short term. They rush from one task to another, never quite recognizing which is most important to their agency's larger objectives. Though they may work hard and have good intentions, they fail to see the big picture and, thus, add little value to their organization or the functions

they manage. Then there are high-impact managers. These managers see the big picture. They know how to manage operational practices and execute tactical goals to support strategic initiatives. They add value to their organization and thus elevate their position from that of an intermediary to key player.

There is an almost magical synergy in a work environment when high-impact managers operate at peak efficiency. Their questions are timely and on target; their ideas are provocative in ways that help move the work forward. They know how to think and act strategically. Transitions from one task to the next seem choreographed. As they walk through the office, their demeanor is calm but they have a sense of urgency. Busy, focused, and driven, these managers produce results and imbue the workplace with energy. Those who watch these managers may feel motivated or intimidated—but they are not unaffected.

Have you ever had a day like that? If you have, you undoubtedly know that it is something that you don't think about as it is occurring—it just happens. When at the top of your game, you are not likely to think about what you are doing or how you are doing it. Middle managers who internalize the High-Impact Management System in their own way and style will enjoy the flow experience more often than many of their peers. Why? High-impact management is designed with several important elements of flow in mind—including fun, challenge, excitement, contribution, and focus. Sound familiar? These are also common intrinsic motivators.

To produce maximum managerial flow, you will want to ensure that you love your job and are feeling the sense of accomplishment and satisfaction that comes with having impact and making a difference. You will want to have fun with your work! So please use these techniques in the way that works best for you.

You likely have noticed that there are two types of suggestions offered in this book. First, and foremost, there are beliefs, mindsets, and ways of thinking. Second, the system offers pragmatic tools and practices suggested by the high-impact management belief set—or definition of success. To begin internalizing the system, take on some of the beliefs and try them. Often, the techniques will easily follow from holding these beliefs.

Where should you begin? The most important suggestion for how to get started is to get started! Getting into action and trying the High-Impact Management System is more important than how you do it or with which technique you begin. Because the system elements support and reinforce one another, it does not matter where you start. Just start.

Keeping the High-Impact Management System Top of Mind: The Scorecard

Regularly reviewing the beliefs and practices will help you internalize the system. As presented in chapters 2 and 5, clarifying goals and communicating them to others improves performance. Middle managers who clarify their personal management development goals and refer to them often will outperform managers who set and then forget about goals. The High-Impact Management Scorecard is a synopsis of the system's elements and techniques. An 8½-x-11-inch version of the High-Impact Management Scorecard is available for download at www.lisahaneberg.com.

How to Use the Scorecard

Middle managers can begin to put these methods and tools to work for them by reviewing the scorecard at the beginning of each day. In time, application of the summarized gems found on the scorecard will become second nature. This will enable the middle manager to access the tools more readily, recognize opportunities for putting high-impact management to work for him or her, and encourage the flow experience.

Using the ROR Cheat Sheet as a Tool for Breakthroughs

On the back of the scorecard is a reprint of the results-oriented responses, or RORs, as presented in chapter 1. This ROR Cheat Sheet can help middle managers diagnose potential response problems and opportunities for specific problem areas such as a project that has stalled or a problem that won't go away.

The ROR Cheat Sheet works by prompting you to think about how you have been approaching a particular problem and will offer potential alternative approaches. Teams can use the cheat sheet to help them solve problems and implement improvements. The cheat sheet is also a good reference for staff or planning meetings.

Conclusion: It Is Just the Beginning!

Honing one's craft is a satisfying and fruitful endeavor. It takes time, commitment, and a passion for the work. Each new idea, skill, method, experience, and tool adds to the high-impact manager's knowledge bank and allows him or her to develop his or her own brand of management. Middle management growth and development is a rich and tailored process that provides organizations with the diverse and creative talent they need to prosper. The objective of the High-Impact Management System is to add to your cache of methods for dealing with complexity, setbacks, and possibilities. Of course, each middle manager will interpret this book differently and take different things from it.

Some may strive for sameness, but differences are what energize the field of management. Whereas diversity of thought, action, and approach benefit organizations, there are basic propositions that underlie the individual approaches of the most successful middle managers—those referred to here as high-impact managers. These propositions are presented and reinforced throughout this book. Therefore, while you should follow your individual path for using the techniques, keep these things in mind:

- High-impact managers are driven to make things better. They know that their roles exist to move work forward in ways that would not occur without them.
- Successful middle managers are proactive. There is simply too much going on every day, and reactive managers cannot accomplish the needed work.
- High-impact managers know they are important and make a difference. They take their roles seriously and possess

professionalism commensurate with these roles. They know they are role models and the perpetuators of the organization's culture.

- High-impact managers believe that the most important work they do is management. They measure accomplishment in terms of management successes in addition to numbers of widgets produced.

- Managers don't control people, and control-oriented performance management approaches can never maximize individual performance. High-impact managers have learned to temper their need to control people and instead focus on controlling their own behaviors, as well as departmental processes and systems.

- Employees, peers, and managers want their middle managers to be at their best and to continue developing new skills. Conventional thinking might lead managers to believe that as they move up the agency's food chain, they have less to learn and do not need as much coaching. High-impact managers have figured out that this is not true. To provide the value and contribution the organization and team members seek, middle managers need to learn more and receive more coaching than they did while they were frontline supervisors. The middle manager's job is different, and the scope of responsibility is immense.

- High-impact managers know that one of the most important choices they make each day is how to spend their precious time.

These themes are common among the best middle managers and run throughout the High-Impact Management System. They are embedded in the guiding principles and can be found as elements of the dozens of techniques and tools offered here. High-impact managers have figured out what they need to do to maximize short-term and long-term results, and they do these things. Their work is successful and fruitful. High-impact managers cover a lot of ground in their organizations. Therefore, the middle manager's breadth of responsibility is significant, and the best have learned how to have an impact on results across the organization.

Senior executives expect their middle managers to influence every level of the organization, and high-impact management will help middle managers effectively reach the people and processes that need their attention and guidance.

This book seeks to reveal the compelling and intriguing elements of the middle manager's job, so that current middle managers will appreciate the work they do, and those not currently in the field will want in. Professionals interested in making a significant contribution to their organization and gaining great satisfaction from their work know that being a middle manager can provide these rewards.

Please use this book often and as a reference. Good luck as you hone your middle management craft. Enjoy the path and the destination, for the ride can be just as invigorating as the finish. Here's to experiencing the magic and flow of high-impact management!

You are all superheroes to me.

Appendix:
Additional Resources
and Recommended Reading

Resources from the Author

These high-impact management resources can be found at www.lisa haneberg.com (click on "My Books"):

- *The High-Impact Management Scorecard* contains many of the key points made in this book. It is an at-a-glance version of the High-Impact Management System.
- *The ROR (Results Oriented Responses) Cheat Sheet* is a wonderful tool that will help middle managers and others assess how to breathe new life into a problem or opportunity. Specific information about the scorecard can be found in chapter 12. Specific information about RORs can be found in chapter 1.
- *The High-Impact Management Definition of Success Cheat Sheet* summarizes several powerful middle management beliefs. Middle managers who choose to take on these beliefs will improve their effectiveness and may produce a breakthrough. This cheat sheet allows middle managers to modify or add to the listed beliefs to create a customized definition of success. Specific information about this tool can be found in chapter 2.
- *The High-Impact Management Playbook* is a planning and communication tool for middle managers that combines goal setting, work planning, and prioritization. The playbook gets its inspiration from sports playbooks. Specific information about this tool can be found in chapter 5.

- *The High-Impact Management Reputation Survey* is a tool middle managers can use to learn more about the reputation they have built in their organization. Specific information about this tool can be found in chapter 4.
- *The Time Audit* is a great tool to help you determine if you are spending your precious time on what matters most. Specific information about this tool can be found in chapter 9.

Recommended Reading for Middle Managers

Abolishing Performance Appraisals: Why They Backfire and What to Do Instead, by Tom Coens and Mary Jenkins. Berrett Koehler.

Beyond Boredom and Anxiety, by Mihaly Csikszentmihalyi. Jossey-Bass.

Circle of Innovation, by Tom Peters. Alfred A. Knopf.

Control Your Destiny or Someone Else Will: Lessons in Mastering Change, by Noel M. Tichy and Stratford Sherman. HarperInformation.

Critical Chain, by Eliyahu M. Goldratt. North River Press.

Deming and Goldratt: The Theory of Constraints and the System of Profound Knowledge, by Domenico Lepore and Oded Cohen. North River Press.

Direct from Dell: Strategies that Revolutionized an Industry, by Michael Dell with Catherine Fredman. HarperBusiness.

The Empowered Manager: Positive Political Skills at Work, by Peter Block. Jossey-Bass.

The Essential Drucker: The Best of Sixty Years of Peter Drucker's Essential Writings on Management, by Peter Drucker. HarperBusiness.

Execution: The Discipline of Getting Things Done, by Larry Bossidy, Ram Charan, and Charles Burck. Crown Publishing Group.

The Fifth Discipline, by Peter Senge. Currency.

Flight of the Buffalo: Soaring to Excellence, Learning to Let Employees Lead, by Ralph Stayer and James Belasco. Warner Books.

The Goal: A Process of Ongoing Improvement, by Eliyahu M. Goldratt and Jeff Cox. North River Press.

Good to Great: Why Some Companies Make the Leap . . . and Others Don't, by Jim Collins. HarperCollins.

How to Win Friends and Influence People, by Dale Carnegie, Dorothy Carnegie, and Arthur R. Pell. Pocket Books.

Implementing Your Strategic Plan: How to Turn "Intent" into Effective Action for Sustainable Change, by C. Davis Fogg. Amacom.

It's Your Ship: Management Techniques from the Best Damn Ship in the Navy, by Captain D. Michael Abrashoff. Warner Books.

Learning Organizations: Developing Cultures for Tomorrow's Workplace, edited by Sarita Chawla and John Renesch. Productivity Press.

Management: Tasks, Responsibilities, Practices, by Peter Drucker. Harper & Row.

Managing Transitions: Making the Most of Changes, by William Bridges. Addison-Wesley.

Masterful Coaching: Extraordinary Results by Impacting People and the Way They Think and Work Together, by Robert Hargrove. Jossey-Bass.

Maverick: The Success Story Behind the World's Most Unusual Workplace, by Ricardo Semler. Warner Books.

No Contest: The Case Against Competition, by Alfie Kohn. Houghton Mifflin.

Nuts! Southwest Airlines' Crazy Recipe for Business and Personal Success, by Kevin Freiberg and Jackie Freiberg. Bard Press.

Out of the Crisis, by W. Edwards Deming. MIT Press.

Punished by Rewards: The Trouble with Gold Stars, Incentive Plans, A's, Praise, and Other Bribes, by Alfie Kohn. Houghton Mifflin.

Reengineering Management: The Mandate for New Leadership, by James Champy. HarperBusiness.

Reengineering the Corporation: A Manifesto for Business Revolution, by Michael Hammer and James Champy. HarperBusiness.

Secrets of Executive Success: How Anyone Can Handle the Human Side of Work and Grow Their Career, by Mark Golin, Mark Bricklin, Dave Diamond, and the Rodale Center for Executive Development. Rodale Press.

Seven Habits of Highly Effective People, by Stephen R. Covey. Simon & Schuster.

Skilled Facilitator: Practical Wisdom for Developing Effective Groups, by Roger Schwarz. Jossey-Bass.

The Social Construction of Reality: A Treatise in the Sociology of Knowledge, by Peter L. Berger and Thomas Luckman. Anchor Books.

Stewardship: Choosing Service or Self-Interest, by Peter Block. Berrett Kohler.

Topgrading: How Leading Companies Win by Hiring, Coaching, and Keeping the Best People, by Bradford D. Smart. Prentice Hall.

Thriving on Chaos: Handbook for a Management Revolution, by Tom Peters. Harper & Row.

What the CEO Wants You to Know: How Your Company Really Works, by Ram Charan. Crown Publishing Group.

Online Site Resources for Middle Managers

Lisa Haneberg's website, www.lisahaneberg.com. Also check out her blog, Management Craft, at www.managementcraft.com.

Great Weblogs (Blogs)

800-CEO-READ Blog, http://800ceoread.com/blog/

Agile Management Blog, www.agilemanagement.net/Articles/Weblog/blog .html

Cranky Middle Manager, www.crankymiddlemanager.com

Fast Company's blog, www.fastcompany.com/

Genuine Curiosity, www.genuinecuriosity.com/genuinecuriosity/

HR Capitalist, www.hrcapitalist.com/

Johnnie Moore, www.johnniemoore.com/blog/

Management Issues, www.management-issues.com/default.asp

Management Skills, www.managementblog.org/

Manager Tools, www.manager-tools.com/

Phil Gerbyshak, www.philgerbyshak.com/

Ramblings from a Glass Half Full, www.terrystarbucker.com/

Seth Godin, http://sethgodin.typepad.com/seths_blog/

Slacker Manager, www.bizzia.com/slackermanager/

Slow Leadership, www.slowleadership.org/blog/

Talking Story with Say Leadership Coaching, www.sayleadershipcoaching .com/talkingstory/

You Already Know This Stuff, http://youalreadyknowthisstuff.blogspot.com/

Other Websites

www.hbr.com: *Harvard Business Review* online. Download and purchase articles on almost any management or leadership topic.

www.fortune.com: Online home of *Fortune* magazine. Always interesting and allows for searching of old articles.

www.fastcompany.com: Website for *Fast Company* magazine, which is one of the more creative and innovative business magazine available to middle managers.

http://800ceoread.com/: A terrific place to find information about business books.

www.personalitypage.com: This is an online assessment that measures behavioral style, similar to the Meyers Briggs Type Indicator. Learn more about natural preferences here.

www.tompeters.com: Tom Peters's website always has lots of interesting information. He is still thought provoking after all these years!

www.pfdf.org: Peter F. Drucker Foundation for Nonprofit Management.

www.businessweek.com: *Business Week* online magazine.

online.wsj.com: *The Wall Street Journal* online.

www.business2.com: *Business 2.0* online magazine.

Tell Me What You Think

I would like your feedback! The High-Impact Management System has been a labor of love developed over the last 20 years. It will continue to expand and improve over time and as new techniques are tested and proved to be effective. Please drop me an email message at lhaneberg@gmail.com. Your opinions are important and valued. Thank you for your feedback!

About the Author

Lisa Haneberg has taught and coached hundreds of managers during the past 25 years including city middle managers, hotel managers, power tool manufacturing department leaders, paper mill union presidents, microchip fabrication shift managers, distribution center leaders, ship captains, division vice presidents, and corporate presidents. Each has benefited from the straightforward solutions to common management maladies that she offers. As a manager, management trainer, and coach for organizations both large and small, she has held leadership positions focused on manager development and effectiveness. Her expertise includes one-to-one management coaching, management course facilitation, organization development, and business writing. She is the vice president and organizational development practice leader for MPI Consulting (www.managementperformance.com). Management is her passion. She is an avid speaker, trainer, and blogger. Find her online at www.managementcraft.com and www.lisahaneberg.com. Her other books include *High Impact Middle Management* (Catalyst, 2008); *Organization Development Basics* (ASTD Press, 2005); *Coaching Basics* (ASTD Press, 2006); *Focus Like a Laser Beam: 10 Ways to Do What Matters Most* (Jossey Bass, 2006); *Two Weeks to a Breakthrough: How to Zoom Toward Your Goal in 14 Days or Less* (Jossey Bass, 2007); *10 Steps to Be a Successful Manager* (ASTD Press, 2007); *Developing Great Managers: 20 Power Hours* (ASTD Press, 2008); and *Hip and Sage: Staying Smart, Cool and Competitive in the Workplace* (Davies Black and ASTD Press, 2009).

Index

Note: *e* represents an exercise, *f* represents a figure, and *t* represents a table.

A

accomplishments, 32–33, 90–91
accountability, 25
actions, 10, 11, 19, 20*f,* 21
ad hoc coaching, 150–52, 157–58
agendas, hidden, 79–80, 88–89
agreements, 46
alignment
   departmental, 93–94
   organizational, 95–103
alliances, 80
Amazon, 140–41, 157
analyses, 88
arguments, 37
audits, 136–37, 138*e,* 139

B

bad-mouthing, 38
balance, work/life, 143
barriers, 66–67, 126
   See also mucky-muck
battles, 86–87
behaviors, 10, 11, 23*e*–24*e,* 81
   See also mucky-muck
beliefs
   actions and, 10, 19, 21
   behaviors and, 23*e*–24*e*
   belief-action cycle, 20*f*
   examination of, 21
   failure and, 27–29
   of success, 21–22, 25–27
Bell Atlantic, 156–57

benchmarks, 44–45
Beyond Boredom and Anxiety
   (Csikszentmihalyi, Mihaly), 167
Black & Decker, 5–6
blame, 38–39, 77
bottlenecks
   constraints vs., 120, 121*f,* 122–23
   throughput and, 107–8, 108*f,* 109*f*
brainstorms, 69–71
breakdowns, system, 114
breakthroughs, 164–65
burned bridges, 38, 80–81

C

challenges, ownership of, 38–39
change-resistant employees, 83–84
changes, 89–90, 115
clean slate creativity, 97–99
coachability
   breakthroughs and, 164–65
   definition of, 159–60
   improvement of, 163–64
   as state of mind, 161–62
   success and, 162–63, 165–66
coaches, 53–54
coaching
   about, 147–49, 148*f,* 150
   types of, 150–54, 156–58
collaboration, 31–32
   See also partnerships; teamwork
communication
   bad-mouthing, 38
   group defections and, 84
   of High-Impact Management
      Playbook, 67

communication *(continued)*
  miscommunication, 76
  overcommunication, 88
  in partnerships, 38
  sabotage through, 84–85
  styles and clashes in, 81
  teams and, 31–33, 35–36, 57, 60–61
  undiscussables and, 77–78
  victim mentality and, 135–36
concerns and barriers, 66–67
conflicts, 37
congestion, 107–8, 108*f*, 109*f*
connections, 110–11, 110*f*
constraints, 108–10, 109*f*, 120–23, 121*f*
constraints, theory of, 119
control, 36–37
co-owning, 34
counseling, 148*f*
creativity, 25, 83–84, 97–99
credits. *See* successes
Critical Chain (Goldratt, Eli), 119
critical paths, 111–12, 112*f*, 113*f*,
  123–24
critical thinking, 35
criticisms, 48–49, 50*e*–51*e*, 52
Csikszentmihalyi, Mihaly, 167

D
data contradictions, 82
defections, 84
Dell, Michael, 18, 162–63
Dell Computer Corporation, 18,
  162–63
departmental alignment, 93–94
departments, 69–73, 86, 96–97,
  99–100
DeWalt, 5–6
Direct from Dell (Dell, Michael), 18,
  162–63
discussions. *See* communication
disempowerment, 81–82
disorganization, 79
duplication of efforts, 83

E
efforts, 83, 87–88
80/20 rule, 15–16, 117–19, 121,
  126–27, 141–43
employees, 79, 83–84, 115
empowerment, 81–82
energy, focus of, 87–88
environments, 89, 116–17, 140–41
errors, 114
excitement, 9
executive coaches, 53–54

F
facilitators, 53–54
failures, 27–29, 35, 114
Federal Express, 18–19
feedback, 48–49, 50*e*–51*e*, 52–54
Flight of the Buffalo (Stayer, Ralph), 18,
  28
follow ups, 88
follows throughs, 46
formal coaching, 152–54, 157

G
goals
  contributions to, 25
  departmental, 96–97
  exercise on, 28
  in High-Impact Management
    Playbook, 64–65
  performance and, 44–45, 58–60
  shared, 34
  sports and, 63
  in strategic plans, 72
  teams and, 57
  See also results
Goldratt, Eli, 119
group defections, 84
guiding principles, 9–11

H
handoffs, 110–11, 110*f*
helplessness, 79
hidden agendas, 79–80, 88–89

high-impact management
  advantages of, 3
  belief-action cycle, 20*f*
  beliefs, actions in, 19, 21
  coaching in, 150
  results-oriented responses (RORs)
    and, 11, 13*t*–14*t*
  role of, 7–9, 8*f*
  time management techniques for,
    136–46
High-Impact Management Playbook,
  63–69, 65*f*
High-Impact Management Scorecard,
  169
High-Impact Management System,
  9–11, 15–16
high-impact managers
  at Black & Decker, 5–6
  definition of, 1–2
  example of, 31–32
  partnership techniques for, 36–40
  reputations and, 54–55
  success and, 22, 25–27, 170–72
  success stories of, 17–19
homework, 86

I
inclusion, 35–36, 88
inefficiencies, 84
information contradictions, 82
Intel, 140–41, 156

J
Johnsonville Foods, 17–18

K
knowledge and reputations, 47

L
laughter, 90
learned helplessness, 79
life/work balance, 143
lighten up, 90

M
management, 10–11, 25, 130–35,
  136–46, 143
managers. *See* high-impact managers;
  middle managers
Maverick (Semler, Ricardo), 143
measurements of performance, 58–60
metrics in High-Impact Management
  Playbook, 65–66
  See also performance
middle managers
  examples of, 32, 43–44, 105–6
  processes and, 94–95
  role of, 6–7, 7*f*
  types of, 1–2, 167–68
miscommunication, 76
  See also communication
models, organization, 97–99
motivations, 39–40, 88–89, 168
mucky-muck
  definition of, 75
  productivity and, 91–92
  techniques for, 85–91
  types of, 76–85
  See also barriers

N
needs, 39–40, 99–100

O
objectives, 72
observations, 52–53, 57
open-ended questions, 56, 88–89,
  154–56
optimism, 90–91
organization, 79, 89–90
organization models, 97–99
organizational alignment, 95–103
organizational structure, 94–95
outcomes. *See* results
overcommunication, 88
  See also communication
ownership, 25, 34, 38–39

P

pace, 140–41
Pareto, Vilfredo, 15–16
Pareto Principle, 15–16
partnerships
  advantages of, 40–41
  case studies of, 40
  importance of, 32–33
  techniques for, 36–40
  traits of, 33–36
  See also collaboration; teamwork
peers, 37, 39–40
performance, 43–45, 58–61
pessimism, 90–91
planning, 129–30, 145–46
playbooks, 63–69, 65*f*
pockets of time, 144–45
politics, 76–77
post-mortem, 28
principles, 9–11
proactivity, 25
problems
  diagnosing, 117–19
  ownership of, 38–39
  solving, 35, 98, 119, 121*f*, 126
processes
  breakdowns in, 114
  evaluation of, 133
  in organizational structure, 94–95
  restructuring of, 102–3
  throughput and, 110–11, 110*f*
procrastination, 132, 134
productivity, 66, 81–82, 84–85, 89–90,
  91–92
projects, 28, 66
promises and reputations, 46
purpose, shared, 34

Q

questions, 56, 88–89, 126–27, 154–56

R

realignment, 95–103
reality checks, 45

relationships
  burning bridges in, 38, 80–81
  case studies of, 40, 54
  management and, 25
  partnerships and, 37
  repairing, 89
  results and, 10
reputations
  case studies of, 54
  self-assessment of, 46–49, 50*e*–51*e*,
    52–55
  team assessment of, 55–57
respect, 35
results
  belief-action cycle, 20*f*
  beliefs, actions and, 19, 21
  maximization of, 106–7
  ownership of, 34
  performance and, 58–60
  relationships and, 10
  reputations and, 46
  teamwork and, 32–33
  See also goals; throughput
results-oriented environment, 116–17
results-oriented responses (RORs)
  application of, 12, 14–15, 25
  cheat sheet for, 13*t*–14*t*, 169–70
  definition of, 11
role models, 25, 31–32

S

sabotage, 84–85
self-assessment, 46–49, 50*e*–51*e*, 52–55
self-talk, 21
Semler, Ricardo, 143
seriousness, 90
skills deficiencies, 112, 114
skills development, 124–25
Smith, Fred, 18–19
Smith, Raymond, 156–57
social functions, 25, 67
  See also communication; relationships
Socratic questions, 154–56
sports, 63

Stayer, Ralph, 17–18, 28, 142–43
sticks-in-the mud, 83–84
strategic plans, 69–73, 86
styles, clashes in, 81
successes
    beliefs and, 21–22, 25–27
    coachability and, 162–63, 165–66
    definition of, 21–22, 26, 27–29
    high-impact managers and, 22,
        25–27, 170–72
    shared, 35, 39
surveys, 48–49, 50*e*–51*e*, 52, 53–54

T
targets. *See* goals
tasks, 66
teams, 55, 57, 60–61
teamwork
    case studies of, 40
    communication and, 31–33, 35–36,
        57
    results and, 32–33
    See also partnerships
The Goal, It's Not Luck (Goldratt, Eli),
    119
theory of constraints, 119
third parties, 53–54
360-degree feedback instruments,
    53–54
throughput
    change and, 115
    examples of, 105–6
    improvement of, 116–27
    maximization of, 106–7
    reductions of, 107–15, 108*f*, 109*f*,
        110*f*, 112*f*, 113*f*
    See also results
time audits, 136–37, 138*e*, 139
time management, 130–35, 136–46
training, 115
trust, 35, 46
turnover, 115

U
undiscussables, 77–78

V
Verizon, 156–57
victim mentality, 135–36
vision, 72, 96–97

W
waste, 114–15
work environments, 89, 116–17,
    140–41
work flow, 66, 103
work inefficiencies, 84
work/life balance, 143
workloads, 81–82